D1485580

**Gary Wigglesworth** was born in Wakefield, West Yorkshire, and now lives in London with his wife, Caroline. A bookseller for sixteen years, he now works in publishing. Currently his book quiz has a monthly residency at The Betsey Trotwood pub in Farringdon and provides the only monthly book quiz for London's literature lovers.

# The Book Lover's Quiz Book

*Gary Wigglesworth*

ROBINSON

ROBINSON

First published in Great Britain in 2020 by Robinson

1 3 5 7 9 10 8 6 4 2

A CIP catalogue record for this book
is available from the British Library.

ISBN: 978-1-47214-529-1

Typeset in Plantin Light by Hewer Text UK Ltd, Edinburgh
Printed and bound in Great Britain by Clays Ltd, Elcograf S.p.A.

Papers used by Robinson are from well-managed
forests and other responsible sources.

Robinson
An imprint of
Little, Brown Book Group
Carmelite House
50 Victoria Embankment
London EC4Y 0DZ

An Hachette UK Company
www.hachette.co.uk

www.littlebrown.co.uk

For Caroline

# Contents

# Introduction

Hello and welcome to *The Book Lover's Quiz Book*! Thank you for picking it up. I imagine that means you love books and you like questions about books. I like you already. Now, I just wanted to give you an idea of how it came about and just what kind of quiz book it is.

Firstly, I love books. I worked in bookselling for sixteen years and, as any bookseller will tell you, you don't work in bookshops for the money. You work in bookshops because you love to read books, you love talking about books and you love telling other people about the books you've read and loved. I had several roles over the years, but the one thing working in a bookshop always comes back to is the recommendation: the chance to send someone home with a book you know they will love. I now work in publishing, and again I am surrounded by people talking about how much they love to read. I'm still selling books, it's just that now it's to booksellers.

Secondly, I love a quiz. Quizzes are great, aren't they? Especially pub quizzes when you can have a drink and a chat with your friends, plus answer a few questions, maybe even win the odd prize. The only thing is, most pub quizzes have maybe one round on books ... sometimes, if you're lucky. And that's just not enough, is it? Not for me and, I hope, not for you. So, I started writing book quizzes, whole quizzes just about books. I hoped there would be enough people like me who wanted a whole night of questions about lovely books and books alone, and there are. You are not alone, book lover!

This book is pretty similar to those quizzes I do in the wild. In each quiz you'll find fixed rounds and changeable rounds – to keep it fresh. I like quizzes where you can have a guess, quizzes that are fun even if you don't know the answer. So, you'll find a fair amount of multiple-choice questions and rounds with enough hints and clues to help you have a stab at the answers. I also like trivia, an interesting fact or two, and you'll find some of those here (including in the footnotes). I should say that, for the 'SayWhatYouSee' picture round, I usually make those images by cutting and pasting. Not on a computer. I literally cut pictures out and paste them together. For this book I've regressed further to drawing them instead, which was a challenge. I'm not the best artist in the world but I have tried to make them look like the things they are supposed to be. Honest.

Also, if you are in a book group or just want to get a group of fellow book lovers together and play in teams, I have made a generic, downloadable answer sheet you can use – find it at gpwigglesworth.co.uk. Oh and Quiz Number 24 is a Christmas quiz – save that one for then!

I sincerely hope you enjoy the book. If you do, look me up on Twitter and Instagram @GPWigglesworth for details of where my next quiz is, some new questions and those all-important book recommendations.

Happy quizzing, bookworms.

Gary

# Quiz Number 1

**Round 1: This and That . . .** all the questions in this round are worth 1 point except question 10, which is worth 5.

1. **The First Question** – Which of these fictional sleuths was published first: A) Inspector Morse in *Last Bus to Woodstock*, B) Inspector Rebus in *Knots and Crosses* or C) Detective Jack Frost in *Frost at Christmas*?

2. **Anagram** – The anagram is always an author's name: I LACE WORDS

3. **Book Quote** – Can you name the book from which this quote comes? 'The reasonable man adapts himself to the world: the unreasonable one persists in trying to adapt the world to himself. Therefore, all progress depends on the unreasonable man.' Is that from: A) *Brave New World* by Aldous Huxley, B) *Atlas Shrugged* by Ayn Rand, C) *Man and Superman* by George Bernard Shaw or D) *Great Again: How to Fix Our Crippled America* by Donald Trump?

4. Which author's middle name was Kindred?

5. **Odd One Out** – Which of the following is not a real John le Carré novel? A) *The Spy Who Came in from the Cold*, B) *A Perfect Spy*, C) *A Legacy of Spies* or D) *An Officer and a Spy*?

6. **Poetry Corner** – What is the next line? This quiz the poem is 'Slough' by John Betjeman: 'Come, friendly bombs, and fall on Slough! . . .'

7. **Fact or Fiction** –Which of the following is a fact about Dan Brown: A) Dan Brown's first book *Digital Fortress*, published in 1998, was slow to start selling, so Dan took to selling it on QVC where it was a modest success, B) Dan Brown's first creative product was a tape he released entitled *SynthAnimals*, which featured the track 'Happy Frogs' or C) a recently discovered species of amphibian in the great basin in Nevada has been named 'The Da Vinci Toad' as the biologist is a big Dan Brown fan?

8. This 1925 novel has been adapted many times, including for cinema four times, in 1926, 1949, a 1974 version starring Robert Redford and Mia Farrow and most recently in 2013 in a version directed by Baz Luhrmann. It was also made into an opera for the New York Metropolitan Opera in 1999. There have been three ballet versions and even two computer games. Most recently, you could experience it as an immersive theatre experience in London's West End. But can you name the book?

9. **What Year?** – In which year did these literary events take place? If you're playing in teams give a point to whichever team gets nearest. Published this year: Keith Waterhouse's *Billy Liar*, Thomas Pynchon's *V* and Maurice Sendak's *Where the Wild Things Are*. Born this year: Poet Laureate Simon Armitage, Alice Sebold and Donna Tartt. Died this year: Aldous Huxley and C. S. Lewis. Sylvia Plath commits suicide only a month after *The Bell Jar* is published.

10. **Give Me Five** – In the 'Mr Men and Little Misses' series by Roger Hargreaves there are seven Mr Men and Little Misses that begin with the letter T. Name five for 5 points.

**Round 2, Part A) What the Dickens!** – Are these real Dickens characters or what? Say (or write) 'Dickens!' if it's genuine and 'What!' if I made it up. A point for each time you are correct:

11. Mr Gulpidge
12. Mr Dick Swiveller
13. Miss Loretta Slimpickle
14. Mr Bloodboil
15. Mr M'Choakumchild

**Round 2, Part B) Blankety Books** – Find the missing word: there's always a theme and this quiz the theme is . . . one-word film titles. A point for each one you get:

16. *[Blank] Sky* by Kate Atkinson
17. *The [Blank] Writer* by Philip Roth
18. *[Blank] at the Villa* by W. Somerset Maugham
19. *The [Blank] of the Spirits* by Carlos Ruiz Zafón
20. *The Buried [Blank]* by Kazuo Ishiguro

**Round 3, Part A) Two of a Kind** – I will describe a character and then an author. They share the same initials so if you know one it will help you get the other. A point for each you can name:

21. Character: The main female protagonist of Jane Austen's 1813 novel *Pride and Prejudice*; she is the second eldest of the sisters, and falls in love with Mr Darcy. Author: Born five years later in 1818, this British author would only release one novel, *Wuthering Heights* in 1847; she died one year later at the age of thirty.
22. Character: Staying in the nineteenth century, this is the criminal who gives Pip a scare in a graveyard on

Christmas Eve in Charles Dickens's *Great Expectations*. Author: This British writer wrote for the sci-fi comic *2000 AD* in the 1970s before moving across to America to work for DC Comics. He is best known for his graphic novels such as *Watchmen, V for Vendetta* and *Batman: The Killing Joke*.

23. Character: The human character in Douglas Adams's *The Hitchhiker's Guide to the Galaxy* who narrowly escapes the Earth's destruction in the company of Ford Prefect – his friend who had just told the perplexed fellow he is, in fact, an alien, and not from Guildford. Author: The American author of the Pulitzer Prize-winning novel *All the Light We Cannot See* from 2014.

24. Character: I imagine most people know the surname of J. K. Rowling's creation who is the gamekeeper and 'Keeper of Keys and Grounds' of Hogwarts, but do you know his first name? Author: The American-born author who lived in London from 1969 until his death in 2011 and is probably best known for his novels *Riddley Walker* and *The Turtle Diary*.

25. Character: The lead character in Angie Thomas's 2017 bestseller *The Hate U Give*, she was played in the 2018 film version by Amandla Stenberg. Author: The American author of the 'Hunger Games' trilogy; 2020 saw the release of her prequel to the series *The Balled of Songbirds and Snakes*.

**Round 3, Part B) ISBN** – I'll give you the ISBN, you give me the title! Not really … All the answers are one-word book titles that start with the letter I, S, B or N. I'll give you the author and the year, and you give me the title for a point:

26. John Williams 1965 – reissued in 2003
27. Sebastian Faulks 1993

28. Neil Gaiman 1996
29. Veronica Roth 2012
30. Toni Morrison 1987

**Round 4, Part A) Oh, and Thingy . . . Whatsit . . .**
Name the missing member of these groups for a point.

31. It's Enid Blyton's 'Famous Five': Dick, Anne, George and Timmy . . . but who else?
32. The four March sisters from Louisa May Alcott's *Little Women*: Meg, Jo, Amy and who else?
33. 'The Watchmen' from Alan Moore and Dave Gibbons classic graphic novel are Ozymandias, Nite Owl II, The Comedian, Dr Manhattan, Silk Spectre II and who else?
34. In George Orwell's *1984* there are four ministries: the Ministry of Love, the Ministry of Peace, the Ministry of Plenty and which other?
35. We'll finish with the Weasley children from J. K. Rowling's 'Harry Potter' series. They are Ron, Bill, Charlie, Percy, George and Ginny, but who is missing?

**Round 4, Part B) Literature Links and Lists** – Answer these novel conundrums for a point each.

36. Which character connects Sebastian Faulks, Jeffery Deaver and John Gardner?
37. *The Girl with the Dragon Tattoo*, *The Girl Who Played with Fire* . . . what comes next?
38. What is the link between George Saunders's Man Booker winner, John Grisham's kid lawyer, the seventh book in Steve Berry's Cotton Malone novels and the 2018 Booker Prize shortlisted novel by Esi Edugyan?

39. Margaret Atwood, Alice Munro, Emily St John Mandel and Yann Martel were all born in which country?
40. What links C. S. Lewis, Philip Larkin and Aldous Huxley?

Finally, there are six 'SayWhatYouSee' visual representations of novels. Give yourself a point for the author and a point for the title.

Total up your answers and see how many you scored.
    The highest score possible on this quiz is 62.
    Thanks for playing!

# The Answers

1.  A) Inspector Morse, 1975 (Frost, 1984; Rebus, 1987)
2.  Oscar Wilde
3.  C) *Man and Superman*
4.  Philip K. Dick
5.  D) *An Officer and a Spy* (this is a Robert Harris novel)
6.  'It isn't fit for humans now.'
7.  B) Dan Brown did indeed release a tape called *SynthAnimals* (he followed that in 1990 with a CD called *Perspectives*)*
8.  *The Great Gatsby* (by F. Scott Fitzgerald)
9.  1963†
10. Mr Tickle, Mr Topsy-Turvy, Mr Tall, Little Miss Tiny, Little Miss Trouble, Little Miss Twins and Little Miss Tidy
11. Dickens! (from *David Copperfield*)
12. Dickens! (from *The Old Curiosity Shop*)
13. What!
14. What!
15. Dickens! (from *Hard Times*)
16. *Big*
17. *Ghost*

---

\* There were three new species of toad discovered in Nevada's great basin in 2017 but they were named Dixie Valley toad, Railroad Valley toad and Hot Creek toad; the biologist is called Dick Tracy.
† Both Aldous Huxley and C. S. Lewis died on the day J. F. K. was assassinated (22 November 1963).

18. *Up*
19. *Labyrinth*
20. *Giant*
21. Elizabeth Bennet and Emily Brontë*
22. Abel Magwitch and Alan Moore
23. Arthur Dent and Anthony Doerr
24. Rubeus Hagrid and Russell Hoban
25. Starr Carter and Suzanne Collins
26. *Stoner*
27. *Birdsong*
28. *Neverwhere* (*Stardust* was 1999)
29. *Insurgent*
30. *Beloved* (*Sula* was 1973)
31. Julian
32. Beth
33. Rorschach
34. Ministry of Truth
35. Fred (one of the twins)
36. James Bond (all written post-Fleming Bond novels)
37. *The Girl Who Kicked the Hornet's Nest* – completing the original 'Millennium Trilogy' by Stieg Larsson
38. American presidents (and have a bonus point if you said 'Mount Rushmore'): George Saunders's novel is **Lincoln** *in the Bardo*; John Grisham's kid lawyer is **Theodore** Boone (so Theodore Roosevelt); the Steve Berry book is *The **Jefferson** Key*; and Esi Edugyan's novel is **Washington** *Black*
39. Canada
40. They all turned down honours – C. S. Lewis and Aldous Huxley turned down knighthoods and Philip Larkin refused a CBE

* Kate Bush, who had a hit single with 'Wuthering Heights', shares Emily Brontë's birthday – 30 July.

41. *Wolf Hall* (A wolf haul) by Hilary Mantel
42. *Confessions of an English Opium-Eater* by Thomas De Quincey
43. *The Grass is Singing* by Doris Lessing
44. *Dear Zoo* by Rod Campbell
45. *The Well of Loneliness* by Radclyffe Hall
46. *Death in Venice* by Thomas Mann

# Quiz Number 2

**Round 1: This and That . . .** all the questions in this round are worth 1 point except question 10, which is worth 5.

1. **The First Question** – Which of these books was published first: A) *One Flew Over the Cuckoo's Nest* by Ken Kesey, B) *At Swim-Two-Birds* by Flann O'Brien or C) *Three Men in a Boat* by Jerome K. Jerome?

2. **Anagram** – The anagram is always an author's name: A POSTMAN JESTER

3. **Book Quote** – Can you name the book from which book this quote comes? 'It's only because of their stupidity that they're able to be so sure of themselves.' Is it from: A) *A Confederacy of Dunces* by John Kennedy Toole, B) *Starter for 10* by David Nicholls, C) *The Trial* by Franz Kafka or D) *Unspeakable: The Autobiography* by John Bercow?

4. Alice Liddell was the inspiration for which literary character?

5. **Odd One Out** – Which of the following is not a real Dick Francis title: A) *Dead Heat*, B) *The Red Pony*, C) *Whip Hand* or D) *High Stakes*?

6. **Poetry Corner** – What is the next line? This quiz the poem is 'Funeral Blues' aka 'Stop all the clocks' by W. H. Auden: 'Stop all the clocks, cut off the telephone . . .'

7 **Fact or Fiction** – Which of the following is a fact about Will Self: A) Will Self refused to apply to Oxford University claiming he 'would have rather died than

join the Bullingdon Club', B) after finishing education Will Self worked as a road sweeper in London or C) for two years Will Self provided the voice for 'Freddy Fox' in the *Peppa Pig* cartoon series?

8. Which Booker Prize-winning author published crime novels under the pseudonym Dan Kavanagh in the 1980s?

9. **What Year?** – In which year did these literary events take place? If you're playing in teams give a point to whichever team gets nearest. Born this year: Neil Gaiman, Ian Rankin and Helen Fielding. Albert Camus and Neville Shute both pass away. *Lady Chatterley's Lover* by D. H. Lawrence sells 200,000 copies in one day after Penguin is found not guilty of obscenity and so is free to publish. Harper Lee's *To Kill a Mockingbird* is published, as is Dr Seuss's *Green Eggs and Ham*.

10. **Give Me Five** – Can you name five Daphne du Maurier novels for 5 points?

**Round 2, Part A) The Smiths** – Which 'Smith' wrote this? I'll give you the title and the year it was published, and you give me the Smith. A point for each you can name.

11. *White Teeth*, 2000
12. *How to Be Both*, 2014
13. *Just Kids*, 2010
14. *Child 44*, 2008
15. *I Capture the Castle*, 1948

**Round 2, Part B) Blankety Books** – Find the missing word: there's always a theme and this quiz it is . . . drinks. A point for each one you get:

16. *Blackberry [Blank]* by Joanne Harris
17. *Fortunately the [Blank]* by Neil Gaiman

18. *The Little [Blank] Shop of Kabul* by Deborah Rodriguez
19. *A [Blank] and a Squeeze* by Julia Donaldson and Axel Scheffler
20. *The [Blank] House Rules* by John Irving

**Round 3, Part A) Two of a Kind** – I will describe a character and then an author. They share the same initials so if you know one it will help you get the other. A point for each you can name.

21. Character: Sherlock's elder, smarter brother in the books by Arthur Conan Doyle; although he only appears in four stories, he has become an important figure in the Doyle canon. Author: The British author best known for *The Curious Incident of the Dog in the Night-time* from 2003 and *The Porpoise* from 2019.

22. Character: The second son of Lord and Lady Marchmain, this character in *Brideshead Revisited*, by Evelyn Waugh, meets Charles Ryder at Oxford and they develop a deep friendship; he has been played by Anthony Andrews on TV and Ben Whishaw in the big screen version of 2008. Author: The author best known for his historical novels such as *Birdsong*, *Charlotte Gray* and *The Girl at the Lion d'Or*; he also published a James Bond novel, *Devil May Care*, in 2008.

23. Character: The lead male protagonist from Malorie Blackman's *Noughts and Crosses*, he is a 'Nought' who becomes the lover of 'Cross' Sephy Hadley. Author: The British fantasy author, comic-book writer, activist and literary critic whose works include *Un Lun Dun*, *Perdido Street Station* and *Kraken*; he's perhaps best known for *The City and the City* which was filmed for BBC Two in 2018, starring David Morrissey as Inspector Tyador Borlú.

24. Character: Created by John Fante, this character is a semi-autobiographical version of the author; a struggling writer, he appears in four Fante novels, the most well-known being *Ask the Dust*. Author: The British author, playwright and screenwriter who found fame with Peter Cook, Dudley Moore and Jonathan Miller in their show *Beyond the Fringe*; he went on to pen plays such as *The History Boys* and *The Madness of George III* and his books include *The Lady in the Van* and *The Uncommon Reader*.

25. Character: Finally, on a vampire theme, the female lead of Stephenie Meyer's 'Twilight' series. Author: The Irish author of the classic Vampire novel *Dracula*.

**Round 3, Part B) Characters** – I will list some key characters from a book – just name the book for a point and the author for another:

26. Celia, Nettie and Shug Avery – 1982
27. Miles Halter, Chip Martin and Alaska Young – 2005
28. Rupert Campbell-Black, Jake Lovell and Tory Maxwell – 1985
29. Alison Hart, Collette and Morris – 2005
30. Roberta (aka Bobbie), Phyllis, Peter and Perks – 1906

**Round 4, Part A) No Wait, I Have a Better Idea . . . !** Everyone is allowed to change their mind and authors are no exception. Below I've listed the original title of a book and the year it was published. Name the title the book was published under for a point, and the author for another.

31. 'Atticus', 1960
32. 'The Dead Un-dead', 1897
33. 'The Last Man in Europe', 1949

34. 'Tomorrow is Another Day', 1936
35. 'Four and a Half Years of Struggle Against Lies, Stupidity and Cowardice', 1925

**Round 4, B) Literature Links and Lists** – Answer these novel conundrums for a point each:

36. *Catch-22*, *All the Light We Cannot See* and *The English Patient* are all set during which war?
37. What is the link between the authors of *The Day of the Locust*, the (penname used by the) author of *The First Fifteen Lives of Harry August*, John Steinbeck's 1952 book that was made into a 1955 film starring James Dean and Ernest Shackleton's book of exploration published in 1922?
38. What metal connects novels by Donna Tartt, Doris Lessing and Francis Spufford?
39. What comes next in this list: *A Study in Scarlet*, *The Sign of the Four*, *The Hound of the Baskervilles*?
40. What occupation do the main protagonists have in James Hilton's *Goodbye, Mr Chips*, R. F. Delderfield's *To Serve Them All My Days* and *Villette* by Charlotte Brontë?

Finally, there are six 'SayWhatYouSee' visual representations of novels. Give yourself a point for the author and a point for the title.

Total up your answers and see how many you scored.
   The highest score possible on this quiz is 71
   Thanks for playing!

# The Answers

1. C) *Three Men in a Boat*, 1889 (*At Swim-Two-Birds*, 1939; *One Flew Over the Cuckoo's Nest*, 1962)
2. James Patterson
3. C) *The Trial* by Franz Kafka
4. Alice from *Alice's Adventures in Wonderland* by Lewis Carroll
5. B) *The Red Pony* (which is a John Steinbeck novel)
6. 'Prevent the dog from barking with a juicy bone'
7. B) He worked briefly as a road sweeper for the General London Council (he did go to Oxford)
8. Julian Barnes
9. 1960
10. *The Loving Spirit, I'll Never Be Young Again, The Progress of Julius, Jamaica Inn, Rebecca, Frenchman's Creek, Hungry Hill, The King's General, The Parasites, My Cousin Rachel, Mary Anne, The Scapegoat, Castle Dor, The Glass-Blowers, The Flight of the Falcon, The House on the Strand, Rule Britannia* ('The Birds' and 'Don't Look Now' were short stories)
11. Zadie Smith
12. Ali Smith
13. Patti Smith
14. Tom Rob Smith
15. Dodie Smith
16. *Wine*
17. *Milk*
18. *Coffee*
19. *Squash*

20. *Cider*
21. Mycroft Holmes and Mark Haddon*
22. Sebastian Flyte and Sebastian Faulks
23. Callum McGregor and China Miéville
24. Arturo Bandini and Alan Bennett.
25. Bella Swan and Bram Stoker†
26. *The Colour Purple* by Alice Walker
27. *Looking for Alaska* by John Green
28. *Riders* by Jilly Cooper
29. *Beyond Black* by Hilary Mantel
30. *The Railway Children* by Edith Nesbit
31. *To Kill a Mockingbird* by Harper Lee
32. *Dracula* by Bram Stoker
33. *1984* by George Orwell‡
34. *Gone with the Wind* by Margaret Mitchell
35. *Mein Kampf: My Struggle, My Glory* by Adolf Hitler
36. The Second World War
37. Points of the compass: Nathanael **West** wrote *The Day of the Locust*, Claire **North** wrote *The First Fifteen Lives of Harry August* (Claire's real name is Catherine Webb), Steinbeck's novel is ***East*** *of Eden* and Shackleton's book is called simply ***South***
38. Gold: *Goldfinch* by Donna Tartt, *The Golden*

---

* There are many versions of Mycroft – but did you know he's the subject of books co-authored by Kareem Abdul-Jabbar? That's Kareem Abdul-Jabbar, the famous basketball player, or you may remember him as the co-pilot Roger Murdock in the film *Airplane!*.

† Best known to us for *Dracula*, in his lifetime Stoker was better known for being the business manager of famous nineteenth-century actor Sir Henry Irving.

‡ The publication date is a clue here, sort of, as Orwell wrote the book in 1948 and switched the digits for the title. But it was published the following year.

*Notebook* by Doris Lessing and *Golden Hill* by Francis Spufford

39. *The Valley of Fear*: these are the four Sherlock Holmes novels by Arthur Conan Doyle in order of publication
40. They are all teachers
41. *Ghost Wall* by Sarah Moss
42. *The Blind Assassin* by Margaret Atwood
43. *Moonraker* by Ian Fleming
44. *Billy Liar* by Keith Waterhouse
45. *Catching Fire* by Suzanne Collins
46. *The Human Stain* by Philip Roth

# Quiz Number 3

**Round 1: This and That** . . . all the questions in this round are worth 1 point except question 10, which is worth 5.

1. **The First Question** – Which of these books was published first: A) *We're Going on a Bear Hunt* by Michael Rosen and Helen Oxenbury, B) *We Wear Pants* by Katie Abey or C) *Where the Wild Things Are* by Maurice Sendak?

2. **Anagram** – The anagram is always an author's name: NAMING A LIE

3. **Book Quote** – Can you name the book from which this quote comes? 'You should be kissed and often, and by someone who knows how.' Is that from: A) *Fifty Shades of Grey* by E. L. James, B) *Gone with the Wind* by Margaret Mitchell, C) *Les Liaisons Dangereuses* by Pierre Choderlos de Laclos or D) *King of Clubs* by Peter Stringfellow?

4. Oops! In 2016 *Time* magazine put which man on its list of 100 most read female authors?

5. **Odd One Out** – Which of the following is not a real Inspector Morse novel by Colin Dexter: A) *Death is Now My Neighbour*, B) *The Wench is Dead*, C) *Death on the River Cam* or D) *The Dead of Jericho*?

6. **Poetry Corner** – What is the next line? This quiz the poem is 'I Wandered Lonely as a Cloud' by William Wordsworth: 'I wandered lonely as a cloud . . .'

7. **Fact or Fiction** – Which of the following is a fact about Martin Amis: A) in his youth Amis attempted to distance himself from his father (Kingsley) and

literature in general by pursuing a career in wrestling, his name was 'The Bullet', B) in 1982 Amis published a guide to arcades and gaming called *Invasion of the Space Invaders* or C) as a child Amis appeared in an episode of *Z-Cars* playing a runaway who was caught shoplifting by 'Fancy' Smith (Brian Blessed)?

8. This book was first published in 1939 and filmed in 1940 by John Ford, starring Henry Fonda. Since then it has been staged many times and was also turned into an opera in 2007. It has also influenced some famous musicians: both Woody Guthrie and Bruce Springsteen have songs that feature the central character's name (Tom Joad). But can you name the book?

9. **What Year?** – In which year did these literary events take place? If you're playing in teams give a point to whichever team gets nearest. Published this year: Anita Brookner's *Hotel du Lac*, Tom Clancy's *The Hunt for Red October* and Martin Amis's *Money*. Journalist and author of 'Chavs' Owen Jones is born while Truman Capote, J. B. Priestley and John Betjeman die this year. *Of Mice and Men* by John Steinbeck is removed from Tennessee libraries – the School Board Chair promises to remove all ostensibly filthy books from public school curricula and libraries.

10 **Give Me Five** – They were rather overshadowed by the Famous 5 but can you name the members of Enid Blyton's Secret 7? Name five for 5 points.

**Round 2, Part A) Sequels** – I will tell you the sequel title and the year it came out – tell me the author for a point and the first book for another point:

11. *Dr Sleep*, 2013
12. *Porno*, 2002
13. *The Starlight Barking*, 1967

14. *Imperial Bedrooms*, 2010
15. *Charlie and the Great Glass Elevator*, 1972

**Round 2, Part B) Blankety Books** – Find the missing word: there's always a theme and this quiz the theme is ... magazines. A point for each one you get:

16. *Rum [Blank]* by Elmore Leonard
17. *[Blank] and Dust* by Ruth Prawer Jhabvala
18. *The [Blank] Tower* by John Fowles
19. *A Little [Blank]* by Hanya Yanagihara
20. *[Blank] Travelling with a Hamster* by Ross Welford

**Round 3, Part A) Two of a Kind** – I will describe a character and then an author. They share the same initials so if you know one it will help you get the other. A point for each you can name:

21. Character: Sue Townsend's teenager who at the time of his first appearance was 13¾ years old; she went on to write about him right up until *The Prostate Years*. Author: The American playwright who wrote *The Crucible*, *Death of a Salesman* and *A View from the Bridge*; he also married Marilyn Monroe – who starred in *The Misfits* with a screenplay by her husband.

22. Character: This *Game of Thrones* character is the illegitimate son of Eddard or 'Ned' Stark; he has appeared in every book of the series; he was played in the TV series by Kit Harington. Author: The Portuguese author of *Blindness* and *The Gospel According to Jesus Christ*, who won the Nobel Prize in Literature in 1998 and died in 2010 aged eighty-seven.

23. Character: Raymond Chandler's detective that featured in *The Big Sleep* and *The Long Goodbye*. The character has been played by many actors in films over the years including: Humphrey Bogart, Elliott Gould and Robert

Mitchum. Author: The Scottish novelist and screen-writer best known for 'The Lewis Trilogy', 'The China Thrillers' and 'The Enzo Files'.

24. Character: The Scottish schoolteacher created by Muriel Spark in her 1961 novel; she was memorably portrayed on film by Dame Maggie Smith – who won the Oscar for her performance in 1969. Author: The American author of *Giovanni's Room* and *Go Tell it on the Mountain*, whose *If Beale Street Could Talk* was made into a 2018 award-winning film; he was also the subject of the 2016 Raoul Peck documentary, *I Am Not Your Negro*.

25. Character: And finally, the father of Harry Potter's friend Ron and husband to Molly; he is played in the films by Mark Williams. Author: The American author whose debut *The Martian* sold 35,000 self-published Kindle editions in three months, leading to a publishing bidding war in 2014; a film of *The Martian* appeared in 2015.

**Round 3, Part B) Russian Dolls** – The second book's title appears inside the first book's title. Have a point for each book you can name. I will give you the authors names and the initials of the first title:

26. Jack Kerouac OTR and Cormac McCarthy
27. Wade Davis TSATR and D. H. Lawrence
28. David Sedaris MTPOD and David Nicholls
29. Tom Wolfe TBOTV and Roddy Doyle
30. Nevil Shute OTB and Alex Garland

**Round 4, Part A) Books in the Movies** – A point for each correct answer:

31. A child enters a magical world through the pages of a book … in which 1979 book by Michael Ende? It was adapted into a classic children's film by Jim Henson in 1984.

32. In the 2015 film *The Boy Next Door*, Jennifer Lopez's character (a teacher) surprisingly receives a first edition of which book: A) *The Little Prince*, B) *Oliver Twist* or C) *The Iliad*?

33. What are the names of the two bookshops in the film *You've Got Mail*?

34. What was the number of the bookshop on Charing Cross Road that features in the title of the 1970 memoir by Helene Hanff? The book was filmed in 1987 with Anthony Hopkins and Anne Bancroft.

35. In 2008 Brendan Fraser accidentally brought Capricorn to life from the pages of *Inkheart* in the film of the same name, but who wrote the book on which the film was based?

**Round 4, Part B) Literature Links and Lists** – Answer these novel conundrums for a point each:

36. What is next in this list: *Northern Lights*, *The Subtle Knife* . . .?

37. What links *Wise Children* by Angela Carter, *Her Fearful Symmetry* by Audrey Niffenegger and *The God of Small Things* by Arundhati Roy?

38. What appears in the title of books by Paula Hawkins, Eimear McBride and Tracy Chevalier?

39. Can you complete this trilogy by Jeff VanderMeer: *Authority*, *Acceptance* and which other?

40. What is the specific link between Zadie Smith, Siri Hustvedt and Ayelet Waldman?

Finally, there are six 'SayWhatYouSee' visual representations of novels. Give yourself a point for the author and a point for the title.

Total up your answers and see how many you scored.
    The highest score possible on this quiz is 66.
    Thanks for playing!

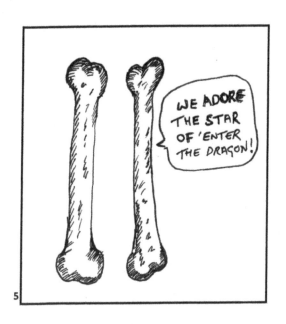

# The Answers

1. C) *Where the Wild Things Are*, 1963 (*We're Going on a Bear Hunt*, 1989, and *We Wear Pants*, 2018)
2. Neil Gaiman
3. B) *Gone with the Wind* by Margaret Mitchell
4. Evelyn Waugh
5. C) *Death on the River Cam*\*
6. 'That floats on high o'er vales and hills'
7. B) He wrote *Invasion of the Space Invaders*†
8. *The Grapes of Wrath* by John Steinbeck
9. 1984
10. Peter, Janet, Jack, Barbara, George, Pam and Colin‡
11. Stephen King, *The Shining*
12. Irvine Welsh, *Trainspotting*
13. Dodie Smith, *The Hundred and One Dalmatians*
14. Brett Easton Ellis, *Less than Zero*
15. Roald Dahl, *Charlie and the Chocolate Factory*
16. *Punch*
17. *Heat*
18. *Ebony*
19. *Life*

\* The Inspector Morse books are set in Oxford; the River Cam is, of course, in Cambridge.
† He did do some acting as a child and appeared in the film *A High Wind in Jamaica*; Amis also ventured into film in 1980 with the screenplay for sci-fi flop *Saturn 3*; Amis has not produced another original screenplay. (If you have seen *Saturn 3* you may understand why.)
‡ Yes, Colin.

20. *Time*
21. Adrian Mole and Arthur Miller
22. Jon Snow and José Saramago
23. Philip Marlowe and Peter May
24. Jean Brodie and James Baldwin
25. Arthur Weasley and Andy Weir
26. *On the Road – The Road*
27. *The Serpent and the Rainbow – The Rainbow*
28. *Me Talk Pretty One Day – One Day*
29. *The Bonfire of the Vanities – The Van*
30. *On the Beach – The Beach*
31. *The Neverending Story*
32. C) *The Iliad**
33. The Shop Around the Corner and Foxbooks
34. 84
35. Cornelia Funke
36. *The Amber Spyglass*: the Philip Pullman 'His Dark Materials' trilogy in publication order
37. They all feature twins
38. Girl: Paula Hawkins, *The Girl on the Train*, Eimear McBride, *A Girl is a Half-formed Thing* and Tracey Chevalier, *Girl with a Pearl Earring*
39. *Annihilation*, from the 'Southern Reach Trilogy'.
40. Their spouses, at time of writing, are also published authors: Zadie Smith is married to Nick Laird, Siri Hustvedt to Paul Auster and Ayelet Waldman to Michael Chabon
41. *Brave New World* by Aldous Huxley
42. *Great Expectations* by Charles Dickens
43. *Fight Club* by Chuck Palahniuk
44. *The Wasp Factory* by Iain Banks
45. *Lovely Bones* (Love (Bruce)Lee Bones) by Alice Sebold
46. *The Night Manager* by John Le Carré

* I did say it was surprising.

# Quiz Number 4

**Round 1: This and That . . .** all the questions in this round are worth 1 point except question 10, which is worth 5.

1. **The First Question** – Which of these books was published first: A) *The Little Prince* by Antoine de Saint-Exupéry, B) *The Princess Bride* by William Goldman or C) *Prince Caspian* by C. S. Lewis?

2. **Anagram** – The anagram is always an author's name: BENT CHIN JOKES

3. **Book Quote** – Can you name the book from which this quote comes? 'If you drink much from a bottle marked "poison" it is certain to disagree with you sooner or later.' Is it from A) *Hangover Square* by Patrick Hamilton, B) *Post Office* by Charles Bukowski, C) *Alice's Adventures in Wonderland* by Lewis Carroll or D) *Celebrate* by Pippa Middleton?

4. Which famous modern-day crime writer has released three standalone novels using the penname Jack Harvey?

5. **Odd One Out** – Which of the following is not a real Arthur Conan Doyle Sherlock Holmes case: 'The Adventure of the Speckled Band', B) 'The Adventure of the Five Red Herrings', C) 'The Adventure of the Engineer's Thumb' or D) 'The Adventure of the Six Napoleons'?

6. **Poetry Corner** – What is the next line? This quiz the poem is 'This Be the Verse' by Philip Larkin: 'They fuck you up, your mum and dad . . .'

7. **Fact or Fiction** – Which of the following is a fact about Samuel Beckett: A) in 1918, Beckett went to serve in the First World War as an ambulance driver in the Italian Army (and was awarded the Italian Silver Medal of Military Valour), B) in 1936 Beckett joined and fought for the Republican army during the Spanish Civil War or C) in 1940, Beckett joined the French Resistance, in which he worked as a courier?

8. Red for drama, orange for fiction, purple for essays, cerise for travel, grey for world affairs, green for crime fiction, dark blue for autobiographies and yellow for miscellaneous – what am I talking about?

9. **What Year?** – In which year did these literary events take place? If you're playing in teams give a point to whichever team gets nearest. Published this year are Jennifer Egan's *A Visit from the Goon Squad* and Suzanne Collins's *Mockingjay*. Neil Gaiman becomes the first author to win both the Carnegie Medal in Literature and the Newbery Medal for *The Graveyard Book*. Jonathan Franzen releases *Freedom* but has his glasses stolen at the launch party at the Serpentine Gallery in London's Hyde Park. Mark Twain's autobiography is officially published as it's 100 years since he dies, and J. D. Salinger passes away at the age of ninety-one.

10. **Give Me Five** – How well do you know the novels of Kurt Vonnegut? Name five for 5 points.

**Round 2, Part A) Musical Monikers** – From which book did these music acts take their names? I will give you the authors' initials as an extra clue. A point for each book named:

11. Josef K were a seminal Scottish post-punk band from the late 1970s and early 1980s but from which novel did they take their name? The author's initials are FK.

12. The Boo Radleys were scouse, psychedelic-leaning Brit poppers who had a big hit with 'Wake Up Boo!', but can you name the source of their name? The author's initials are HL.

13. Steely Dan are an American Jazz rock band founded in the 1970s, but which novel begat their moniker? The author's initials are WB.

14. Level 42: from where did this English, bass-slapping, pop-funk combo from the 1980s (and still going) get their name? The author's initials are DA.

15. Moloko were an electronic duo who took inspiration for their name from which cult bestseller? The author's initials are AB.

**Round 2, Part B) Blankety Books** – Find the missing word: there's always a theme and this quiz the theme is … birds. A point for each one you get:

16. *Jonathan Livingstone [Blank]* by Richard Bach
17. *Flaubert's [Blank]* by Julian Barnes
18. *The [Blank] Tunnel* by John le Carré
19. *Black [Blank]* by Dean Atta
20. *The Cry of the [Blank]* by Patricia Highsmith

**Round 3, Part A) Two of a Kind** – I will describe a character and then an author. They share the same initials so if you know one it will help you get the other. A point for each you can name.

21. Character: The character created by Truman Capote in 1958 in his novella *Breakfast at Tiffany's* who lives with a cat in a New York apartment and was played in the film by Audrey Hepburn. Author: The bestselling American romance author who has written over 150 novels and

novellas, been published in approximately 25 languages and sold over 75 million copies of her work; she also writes under the penname Shannon Drake.

22. Character: The titular character of John Williams's 1965 novel that sold 2,000 copies and went out of print after a year but eventually became a bestseller in 2013 when it was named Waterstones Book of the Year. Author: The Scottish historical author, historian, poet and play-wright born in 1771, probably best known for the novels *Ivanhoe* and *Rob Roy*.

23. Character: The titular character from George Eliot's final novel published in 1876 – the novel begins with this character meeting the other main protagonist, Gwendolen Harleth. Author: The acclaimed American author of *White Noise, Libra, Underworld* and *Cosmopolis* (the film of which starred Robert Pattinson).

24. Character: Another titular character – this time of Stephen King's 1974 debut novel about a telekinetic prom queen who has her revenge. Author: The American author of the bestselling Pulitzer Prize-winning novel *The Underground Railroad* and *The Nickel Boys* from 2019.

25. Character: Finally, the main protagonist from F. Scott Fitzgerald's novel of 1925 set in the fictional towns of West and East Egg. Author: The American author of *The Fault in Our Stars, Looking for Alaska* and *Paper Towns*.

**Round 3, Part B) Awesome Alliterative Authors** – I will give you their date of birth, the title of their first published work and the initial with which their names begin. Just name the author for a point:

26. Born 2 October 1904, first book was *The Man Within*, and the letter is G.

27. Born 1954, first book was *The Restraint of Beasts*, and the letter is M.
28. Born 3 February 1979, first fiction book was *Miss Peregrine's Home for Peculiar Children*, and the letter is R.
29. Born 23 October 1974, first book was *The White Tiger* and the letter is A.
30. Born 17 September 1935, first book was *One Flew Over the Cuckoo's Nest*, and the letter is K.

**Round 4, Part A) Book Bingo** – Get your Mecca daubers out! A point for every correct number you spot:

31. How many people did Eddie meet in Heaven in Mitch Albom's novel of 2003: Just My Age 2 and 1: 21, Dancing Queen 17, Man Alive number 5 or was it the Brighton Line 59?
32. How many minutes are there in the title of Sarah Pinborough's novel of 2016: 2 Little Ducks 22 (quack quack), Knock at the Door number 4, Unlucky for Some 13 or Doctor's Orders number 9?
33. How many thousand streets under the sky are there in Patrick Hamilton's 1935 classic: Boris's Den number 10, Bullseye Blind 50, One Score Blind 20 or Burlington Bertie number 30?
34. How many kinds of loneliness are there in Richard Yates's novel of 1962: Kelly's Eye number 1, Legs 11 (whistle), Tom Mix number 6 or Buckle My Shoe 32?
35. How many killings are there in the title of Marlon James's Man Booker-winning novel of 2014: Lucky for Some number 7, Duck and Dive 25, Garden Gate number 8 or Cup of Tea number 3?

**Round 4, Part B) Literature Links and Lists** – Answer these novel conundrums for a point each:

36. What colour appears in the titles of books by Lucy Maud Montgomery, Fannie Flagg and Anne Enright?
37. This is quite a tricky one. What comes next in this list: *Macbeth* and eight, *Hamlet* and nine, *King Lear* and ten? Half a point for the title and half a point for the number!
38. In which country were all these authors born: Peter Carey, Richard Flanagan, Garth Nix and Liane Moriarty?
39. What links 'Laska' in *Anna Karenina*, 'Pilot' in *Jane Eyre* and 'Jip' in *David Copperfield*?
40. What connects John Irving, Jeremy Clarkson, Jostein Gaarder and Danny Dyer?

Finally, there are six 'SayWhatYouSee' visual representations of novels. Give yourself a point for the author and a point for the title.

Total up your answers and see how many you scored.
     The highest score possible on this quiz is 61.
     Thanks for playing!

# The Answers

1. A) *The Little Prince*, 1943 (*Prince Caspian*, 1951, *The Princess Bride*, 1977)
2. John Steinbeck
3. C) *Alice's Adventures in Wonderland*[*]
4. Ian Rankin
5. B) 'The Adventure of the Five Red Herrings' (*The Five Red Herrings* is a 1931 Lord Peter Wimsey mystery by Dorothy L. Sayers)
6. 'They may not mean to, but they do'
7. C) He joined the French Resistance[†]
8. The classic Penguin Books colour code
9. 2010
10. *Player Piano, The Sirens of Titan, Mother Night, Cat's Cradle, God Bless You, Mr Rosewater, Slaughterhouse-Five, Breakfast of Champions, Slapstick, Jailbird, Deadeye Dick, Galápagos, Bluebeard, Hocus Pocus, Timequake*
11. *The Trial* by Franz Kafka
12. *To Kill a Mockingbird* by Harper Lee
13. *Naked Lunch* by William Burroughs
14. *The Hitchhiker's Guide to the Galaxy* by Douglas Adams

---

[*] Pippa Middleton's book does contain useful advice such as: a really late start warrants brunch in lieu of lunch and don't forget to put a pitcher of water and glasses on the table, or a nearby side table if there's no room.

[†] Though later in his life he described it as 'boy scout stuff'; (A) was Ernest Hemingway; B) was George Orwell.

15. *A Clockwork Orange* by Anthony Burgess*
16. *Seagull*
17. *Parrot*
18. *Pigeon*
19. *Flamingo*
20. *Owl*
21. Holly Golightly and Heather Graham
22. William Stoner and Walter Scott
23. Daniel Deronda and Don DeLillo
24. Carrie White and Colson Whitehead
25. Jay Gatsby and John Green
26. Graham Greene
27. Magnus Mills
28. Ransom Riggs†
29. Aravind Adiga
30. Ken Kesey
31. 5: *The Five People You Meet in Heaven*
32. 13: *13 Minutes*
33. 20: *20,000 Streets Under the Sky*
34. 11: *Eleven Kinds of Loneliness*
35. 7: *A Brief History of Seven Killings*
36. Green: Lucy Maud Montgomery's *Anne of Green Gables*, Fannie Flagg's *Fried Green Tomatoes at the Whistle Stop Café*, Anne Enright's *The Green Road*
37. *Titus Andronicus* and fourteen – it's the number of deaths in individual Shakespeare plays increasing to the most

---

* *A Clockwork Orange* must be the most inspirational book for bands there is. As well as Moloko, there are Heaven 17, Korova Milkbar, Haircut 100, the Malchicks, Campag Velocet . . .
† Riggs's first non-fiction book was *The Sherlock Holmes Handbook: The Methods and Mysteries of the World's Greatest Detective* – but I thought *Miss Peregrine's* . . . gave you more of a chance!

38. Australia
39. They are all dogs
40. They have all published books called *The World According to ...*: John Irving, *The World According to Garp*; Jostein Gaarder, *The World According to Anna*; Jeremy Clarkson and Danny Dyer – *The World According to ...* themselves
41. *The Pelican Brief* by John Grisham
42. *A Portrait of the Artist as a Young Man* by James Joyce
43. *The Silence of the Lambs* by Thomas Harris
44. *The Magic Mountain* by Thomas Mann
45. *Case Histories* by Kate Atkinson
46. *Divergent* (Diver gent) by Veronica Roth

# Quiz Number 5

**Round 1: This and That . . .** all the questions in this round are worth 1 point except question 10, which is worth 5.

1. **The First Question** – Which of these Ian Fleming 'James Bond' books was published first: A) *Casino Royale*, B) *Dr No* or C) *Moonraker*?

2. **Anagram** – The anagram is always an author's name: LOOSELY YARN

3. **Book Quote** – Can you name the book from which this quote comes? 'Whatever our souls are made of, his and mine are the same.' Is it from A) *Wuthering Heights* by Emily Brontë, B) *The Notebook* by Nicholas Sparks, C) *Call Me By Your Name* by André Aciman or D) *Ooh What a Lovely Pair: Our Story* by Ant and Dec?

4. Of which novelist did Katherine Mansfield complain that he 'never gets any further than warming the teapot. He's a rare fine hand at that. Feel this teapot. Is it not beautifully warm? Yes, but there ain't going to be no tea': A) E. M. Forster, B) D. H. Lawrence or C) Charles Dickens?

5. **Odd One Out** – Which of the following is not a real Jilly Cooper novel: A) *Riders*, B) *Jump!*, C) *Hot in the Saddle* or D) *Polo*?

6. **Poetry Corner** – What is the next line? This quiz the poem is 'The Tyger' by William Blake: 'Tyger Tyger, burning bright . . .'

7. **Fact or Fiction** – Which of the following is a fact about Nick Hornby: A) we all know Nick Hornby likes his

football (he wrote *Fever Pitch*, after all), but he also played for his beloved Arsenal FC at youth level, B) we all know Nick Hornby likes his music (he wrote *High Fidelity*, after all), but he also collaborated on an album with Ben Folds of Ben Folds 5 fame or C) we all know Nick Hornby likes erm ... walking (he wrote the screenplay to the movie *Wild*, after all), but he also walked from Land's End to John O' Groats to raise money for charity in 2008?

8. This book was published in 1862. It has been adapted for film six times, the first in 1935 starring Charles Laughton, the latest in 2012 starring Hugh Jackman. There have also been radio adaptations (including one by Orson Welles) and TV versions, the most recent being a BBC adaptation in 2018. But perhaps the most famous adaptation of this book is the musical that premiered in 1980 at the Palais des Sports in Paris and became one of the most successful stage shows ever produced. Can you name the original book?

9. **What Year?** – In which year did these literary events take place? If you're playing in teams give a point to whichever team gets nearest. Published this year: Martin Amis's *London Fields*, Ben Elton's debut *Stark* and Amy Tan's *Joy Luck Club*. Kazuo Ishiguro wins the Man Booker Prize for *The Remains of the Day*. Samuel Beckett and Daphne du Maurier both pass away, and on 14 February the Ayatollah Khomeini issues a fatwa calling for the death of Salman Rushdie and his publishers for the previous year's *The Satanic Verses*.

10. **Give Me Five** – There are over fifty *That's Not My ...* books listed on the Usborne website. At time of writing nine of the subjects begin with 'P'. Name 5 for a point each.

**Round 2, Part A) Sensational Sophomores** – I'll give you the author and the title of their second book: you just tell me the title of their debut for a point:

11. *Pride and Prejudice* by Jane Austen
12. *Something Happened* by Joseph Heller
13. *Walking on Glass* by Iain Banks
14. *The Autograph Man* by Zadie Smith
15. *The Wonderful Visit* by H. G. Wells

**Round 2, Part B) Blankety Books** – Find the missing word: there's always a theme and this quiz the theme is . . . hair and hairstyles. A point for each one you get:

16. *A Street Cat Named [Blank]* by James Bowen
17. *Big [Blanks]* by Howard Goodall
18. *Skeleton [Blank]* by Stephen King
19. *Hunches in [Blanks]* by Dr Seuss
20. *The Last of the [Blanks]* by James Fenimore Cooper

**Round 3, Part A) Two of a Kind** – I will describe a character and then an author. They share the same initials so if you know one it will help you get the other. A point for each you can name:

21. Character: Mark Twain character who first appeared in 1876; he went on to appear in four novels in total, featuring in the title of three; the first book features this character as a young boy growing up next to the Mississippi River. Author: The English satirical author born in 1928 who is best known for his series of 'Wilt' novels, *Porterhouse Blue* and *Blott on the Landscape*.
22. Character: The companion assistant and transcriber of Sherlock Holmes's adventures created by Arthur Conan Doyle. Author: The English author of such sci-fi classics as *The Midwich Cuckoos* and *The Day of the Triffids*.
23. Character: The character in John Steinbeck's classic *Of Mice and Men* who accompanies George Milton in their search for a better future; he is a giant of a man but

slow-witted; his dream is simply to be able to live off the land and tend rabbits. Author: The penname of Daniel Handler, the author of 'A Series of Unfortunate Events'; the books follow the lives of three children, Violet, Sunny and Klaus Baudelaire, who are placed in the care of their murderous relative Count Olaf – who wishes to steal the children's inheritance; Olaf has been played by Jim Carrey and Neil Patrick Harris.

24. Character: The inspector created by Georges Simenon, who first appeared in the 1931 novel *The Strange Case of Peter the Lett*, and went on to appear in seventy-five novels and twenty-eight short stories; he has been played on film by Charles Laughton and on TV by Rupert Davies, Michael Gambon and Rowan Atkinson. Author: The celebrated Spanish author who in 2013 was awarded the Prix Formentor; his novels include: *A Heart So White*, *The Infatuations* and *Thus Bad Begin*.

25. Character: The private detective created by J. K. Rowling, using the penname Robert Galbraith; he is an ex-soldier and lost half of his leg in Afghanistan; he is joined in investigation by his assistant Robin Ellacott; Tom Burke plays this character in the BBC series. Author: The creator of 'Peanuts' – the comic strip that featured Snoopy, Charlie Brown *et al.* that ran for over fifty years and is loved all over the world.

**Round 3, Part B) They Have Their Exits and Their Entrances** – Name the Shakespeare play from its first line for a point:

26. 'Who's there?'
27. 'If music be the food of love, play on'
28. 'When shall we three meet again? In thunder, lightning, or in rain?'

29. 'Now, fair Hippolyta, our nuptial hour draws on apace'
30. 'Two households both alike in dignity'

**Round 4, Part A) Location Location Location** – I'll tell you a location that features in a novel and the year it was published. You tell me the author and the title – a point for each:

31. The Overlook Hotel, 1977
32. Satis House, 1861
33. 124 Bluestone Road, 1987
34. Gormenghast Castle, 1946
35. Toad Hall, 1908

**Round 4, Part B) Literature Links and Lists** – Answer these novel conundrums for a point each.

36. What title links books by Katie Price, Nasser Hussain, Tess Gerritsen, Derek Landy, Peter Robinson, Gordon Ramsay, Nigel Havers and many more!
37. Which city connects the titles of books by Ben Aaronovitch, James Patterson and Mick Herron?
38. What comes next in this list: *The Last Olympian, The Battle of the Labyrinth, The Titan's Curse, The Sea of Monsters*?
39. What TV show connects John Updike, Thomas Pynchon, Stephen King and J. K. Rowling?
40. What could come next in this list: the second Sherlock Holmes novel, Jerome K. Jerome's book about chums on the river, Flann O'Brien's 1939 novel?

Finally, there are six 'SayWhatYouSee' visual representations of novels. Give yourself a point for the author and a point for the title.

Total up your answers and see how many you scored.
    The highest score possible on this quiz is 66.
    Thanks for playing!

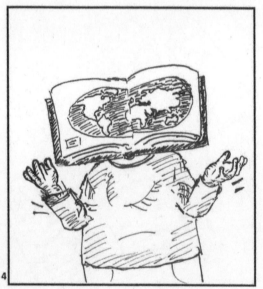

# The Answers

1. A) *Casino Royale*, 1953 (*Dr No*, 1958, Moonraker, 1955)[*]
2. Sally Rooney
3. A) *Wuthering Heights* by Emily Brontë
4. A) E. M. Forster
5. C) *Hot in the Saddle* (which is by Randi Alexander)[†]
6. 'In the forests of the night'
7. B) Nick Hornby wrote the lyrics for the Ben Folds album *Lonely Avenue* in 2010
8. *Les Misérables* by Victor Hugo
9. 1989
10. *Panda, Penguin, Piglet, Pirate, Plane, Polar Bear, Pony, Princess, Puppy*
11. *Sense and Sensibility*
12. *Catch-22*
13. *The Wasp Factory*
14. *White Teeth*
15. *The Time Machine*
16. *Bob*
17. *Bangs*
18. *Crew*
19. *Bunches*
20. *Mohicans*
21. Tom Sawyer and Tom Sharpe

[*] When *Casino Royale* was published in the United States two years later the name was changed to *You Asked for it*.
[†] Book two is called *Badge and a Saddle* and three is called *Saddle and a Siren*.

22. John Watson and John Wyndham
23. Lennie Small and Lemony Snicket
24. Jules Maigret and Javier Marías
25. Cormoran Strike and Charles Schulz
26. *Hamlet*
27. *Twelfth Night*
28. *Macbeth*
29. *A Midsummer Night's Dream*
30. *Romeo and Juliet*
31. *The Shining* by Stephen King
32. *Great Expectations* by Charles Dickens
33. *Beloved* by Toni Morrison
34. *Titus Groan* by Mervyn Peake*
35. *The Wind in the Willows* by Kenneth Grahame
36. *Playing with Fire*
37. London: *Rivers of London* by Ben Aaronovitch, *London Bridges* by James Patterson, *London Rules* by Mick Herron
38. *The Lightning Thief*: these are the Percy Jackson books by Rick Riordan in reverse publication order
39. They've all had cameos in *The Simpsons*
40. Any book with 'one' the title, e.g. *One Day, Ready Player One, One Flew Over the Cuckoo's Nest*: the second Holmes novel is *The Sign of the **Four**,* Jerome K. Jerome's novel is ***Three** Men in a Boat* and O'Brien's novel is *At Swim-**Two**-Birds*
41. *The English Patient* by Michael Ondaatje
42. *Postcards from the Edge* by Carrie Fisher
43. *Vanity Fair* by William Makepeace Thackery
44. *Atlas Shrugged* by Ayn Rand
45. *Hamnet* by Maggie O'Farrell
46. *The Perks of Being a Wallflower* by Stephen Chbosky

* This is the first in the 'Gormenghast' series; *Gormenghast* itself followed in 1950.

# Quiz Number 6

**Round 1: This and That . . .** all the questions in this round are worth 1 point except question 10, which is worth 5.

1. **The First Question** – Which of these authors was born first: A) Washington Irving, B) Lucy M. Boston or C) Tennessee Williams?
2. **Anagram** – The anagram is always an author's name: NINETEEN OTTER JAWS
3. **Book Quote** – Can you name the book from which this quote comes? 'No man, for any considerable period, can wear one face to himself and another to the multitude, without finally getting bewildered as to which may be the true.' Is it from: A) *The Strange Case of Dr Jekyll and Mr Hyde* by Robert Louis Stevenson, B) *The Scarlet Letter* by Nathaniel Hawthorne, C) *American Psycho* by Bret Easton Ellis or D) *Fire and Fury: Inside the Trump Whitehouse* by Michael Wolf?
4. Which is the only Shakespeare play with an English place name in the title?
5. **Odd One Out** – Which of the following is not a real Philippa Gregory novel: A) *The White Queen*, B) *The Traitor Queen*, C) *The Red Queen* or D) *The Other Queen*?
6. **Poetry Corner** – What is the next line? This quiz the poem is 'Now We Are Six' by A. A. Milne: 'When I was one . . .'
7. **Fact or Fiction** – Which of the following is a fact about Neil Gaiman: A) Neil Gaiman is a keen drummer and

once joined the Foo Fighters on stage playing a second drumkit, B) Neil Gaiman's first published book was a biography of 1980s pop act Duran Duran or C) Neil Gaiman worked as a TV extra while at college, even appearing in his favourite show *Doctor Who* (Tom Baker era – the story was 'The Horns of Nimon', Part 3)?

8. Which school did Darrell Rivers and Gwendoline Lacey attend?

9. **What Year?** – In which year did these literary events take place? If you're playing in teams give a point to whichever team gets nearest. *The Luminaries* by Eleanor Catton wins the Man Booker Prize, Donna Tartt's third book *The Goldfinch* is released and J. K. Rowling publishes *The Cuckoo's Calling* under the penname Robert Galbraith. Tom Clancy, Tom Sharpe and Iain Banks all pass away.

10. **Give Me Five** – There are forty-two original 'Thomas the Tank Engine' books by the Reverend Wilbert Awdry and his son Christopher, and twelve have Christian names (not including Thomas) in the titles. Name five for 5 points.

**Round 2, Part A) The Question Is . . .** – The titles of these books are all questions. I will tell you the author, the initial letters of the title and year it was published – just tell me the title for a point:

11. Agatha Christie, 1934, WDTAE
12. Sophie Kinsella, 2008, RM
13. Maria Semple, 2012, WYGB
14. Michael Moore, 2003, DWMC
15. Kate Atkinson, 2008, WWTBGN
15a. Bonus point – why is 13 the odd one out of that list?

**Round 2, Part B) Blankety Books** – Find the missing word: there's always a theme and this quiz the theme is ... fruit . A point for each one you get:

16. *[Blanks] Are Not the Only Fruit* by Jeanette Winterson
17. *The Golden [Blanks] of the Sun* by Ray Bradbury
18. *The [Blank] Thief* by Joanne Harris
19. *The [Blank] Table* by Julian Barnes
20. *What's Eating Gilbert [Blank]* by Peter Hedges

**Round 3, Part A) Two of a Kind** – I will describe a character and then an author. They share the same initials so if you know one it will help you get the other. A point for each you can name.

21. Character: Titular character from Oscar Wilde's only novel, published in 1891; this character sells his soul to remain young and beautiful. Author: An American author who mixes historical fiction, romance and science fiction; she is best known for her 'Outlander' and 'Lord John' series; 'Outlander' was adapted for American television, debuting in 2014.
22. Character: The character who travelled around the world in eighty days in Jules Verne's novel of 1873; he has been portrayed on film by David Niven and Steve Coogan. Author: The English Man Booker Prize-winning author of *Offshore*, *The Golden Child* and *The Bookshop*, which was filmed in 2017, starring Emily Mortimer and Bill Nighy.
23. Character: 'Harry Potter' character also known as 'Padfoot' or 'Snuffles' – he was a pure-blood wizard and a cousin of Bellatrix Lestrange; he was played in the films by Gary Oldman (in a very natty jacket). Author: A Canadian author born in 1915 who won the Pulitzer and the Nobel Prize in Literature, and who is the only

writer to win the National Book Award for fiction three times; his works include *Herzog* and *Humboldt's Gift* and *The Adventure of Augie March*.

24. Character: The child protagonist from R. J. Palacios's novel *Wonder* who suffers from a facial disfigurement; Jacob Tremblay played this character in the 2017 film by Stephen Chbosky (the author of *The Perks of Being a Wallflower*). Author: The English author best known for his twelve-volume work *A Dance to the Music of Time* published between 1951 and 1975; it was adapted into TV mini-series by Channel 4 in 1997.

25. Character: Titular character of Jane Austen's 1815 novel, the last one to be published in her lifetime; the character has been played by Gwyneth Paltrow, Kate Beckinsale (TV) and most recently in the 2020 film by Anna Taylor-Joy. Author: The American Pulitzer Prize-winning author best known for *The Age of Innocence* and *Ethan Frome*.

**Round 3, Part B) Alliterative Titles** – I'll give you the author and the year of publication, you give me the alliterative title for a point:

26. Frank McCourt, 1996
27. George Eliot, 1876
28. Sam Selvon, 1956
29. Richard Yates, 1961
30. Michael Morpurgo, 2003

**Round 4, Part A) Definitive Definition** – One word, three definitions: which is correct? A point for every true definition you spot:

31. And the word is 'Melange' but is it: A) the name of the drug that is central to the plot in Frank Herbert's *Dune*,

B) the name of the chocolate shop opened by Vianne in Joanne Harris's *Chocolat* or C) the name of the butler in *Rebecca* by Daphne du Maurier?

32. And the word is 'Egeon' but is it: A) the name of the corporation that creates replicants in Philp K. Dick's *Do Androids Dream of Electric Sheep?*, B) the name of one of Winnie the Pooh's friends in the Hundred Acre Wood or C) the name of a merchant from Syracuse who appears in Shakespeare's *The Comedy of Errors*?

33. And the word is 'Tolchock' but is it: A) the drug favoured by William Lee, the narrator of William Burroughs's *Naked Lunch*, B) the name of a dog in a short story by Chekhov from 1897 or C) a word used in Anthony Burgess's *A Clockwork Orange* meaning to strike someone?

34. And the word is 'Brobdingnag' but is it: A) a fictional creature created by Lewis Carroll that appears in his poem 'Jabberwocky', B) a fictional land occupied by giants in Jonathan Swift's novel *Gulliver's Travels* or C) one of the dwarves in Thorin's company – the group that Bilbo joins in *The Hobbit* by J. R. R. Tolkien?

35. And the word is 'Alohomora' but is it: A) the name of a witch that appears in *Witches Abroad* from the 'Discworld' series by Terry Pratchett, or B) an unlocking spell used in the 'Harry Potter' series of books by J. K. Rowling or C) the name of Ahab's whaling ship in Herman Melville's *Moby Dick*?

**Round 4, Part B) Literature links and lists** – Answer these novel conundrums for a point each:

36. What colour links books by Thomas Harris, Orhan Pamuk and Hergé?

37. What links these books: *Rebecca* by Daphne du Maurier, *Invisible Man* by Ralph Ellison and *Surfacing* by Margaret Atwood?

38. Which artist and children's author has illustrated books for Roald Dahl, Joan Aiken, Nils-Olof Franzén and Michael Rosen?

39. What comes next in this list: *The Fever Code, The Kill Order, The Death Cure, The Scorch Trials*?

40. What links: a Planet, a Rainbow, Christmas, Daddy, the Past and a Lot and the Bed?

Finally, there are six 'SayWhatYouSee' visual representations of novels. Give yourself a point for the author and a point for the title.

Total up your answers and see how many you scored.

The highest score possible on this quiz is 62.

Thanks for playing!

# The Answers

1. A) Washington Irving, 1783 (Lucy M. Boston, 1892, Tennessee Williams, 1911)
2. Jeanette Winterson
3. B) *The Scarlet Letter* by Nathaniel Hawthorne
4. *The Merry Wives of Windsor*
5. B) *The Traitor Queen* (a book by Trudi Canavan)
6. 'I had just begun'
7. B) His first published book was indeed a biography of Duran Duran in 1984*
8. Malory Towers – from the Enid Blyton series
9. 2013
10. James, Henry, Toby, Gordon, Edward, Percy, Stepney, Oliver, Duke, Jock, Wilbert and Victoria
11. *Why Didn't They Ask Evans?*
12. *Remember Me?*
13. *Where'd You Go, Bernadette*
14. *Dude, Where's My Country?*
15. *When Will There Be Good News?*
15a. The title is a question but it has no question mark
16. *Oranges*
17. *Apples*
18. *Strawberry*

* Neil Gaiman's second published book was *Don't Panic: The Official Hitchhiker's Guide to the Galaxy Companion* in 1988. His first fiction was *Good Omens* co-authored with Terry Pratchett in 1990.

19. *Lemon*
20. *Grape*
21. Dorian Gray and Diana Gabaldon
22. Phileas Fogg and Penelope Fitzgerald
23. Sirius Black and Saul Bellow
24. August 'Auggie' Pullman and Anthony Powell
25. Emma Woodhouse and Edith Wharton
26. *Angela's Ashes*
27. *Daniel Deronda*
28. *The Lonely Londoners*
29. *Revolutionary Road*
30. *Private Peaceful*
31. A) Melange is the name of the drug used in *Dune*; it's often known as 'the Spice'*
32. C) Egeon is a merchant from Syracuse†
33. C) Tolchock appears in *A Clockwork Orange*
34. B) It is a land in *Gulliver's Travels*
35. B) It is an unlocking spell from the 'Harry Potter' series
36. Red: *Red Dragon* by Thomas Harris, *My Name is Red* by Orhan Pamuk, *Red Rackham's Treasure* by Hergé
37. They all have unnamed narrators
38. Quentin Blake
39. *The Maze Runner*: they are James Dashner's 'Maze Runner' series in reverse publication order
40. All things *The Dinosaur that Pooped* ... has pooped (from books by Tom Fletcher and Dougie Poynter of McFly)
41. *The Heart is a Lonely Hunter* by Carson McCullers

---

* There is an actual Melange chocolate shop but it's in Peckham; the shop in *Chocolat* is called La Céleste Praline.
† In the film *Blade Runner*, the corporation's name is the Tyrell Corporation – Dick doesn't mention a corporation name in the book.

42. *Poor Cow* by Nell Dunn
43. *Alone in Berlin* (a loan in Berlin) by Hans Fallada
44. *Hangover Square* by Patrick Hamilton
45. *Journey to the Centre of the Earth* by Jules Verne
46. *Bluebeard* by Kurt Vonnegut

# Quiz Number 7

**Round 1: This and That . . .** all the questions in this round are worth 1 point except question 10, which is worth 5.

1. **The First Question** – Which of these Thomas Harris books was published first: A) *Hannibal*, B) *Red Dragon* or C) *The Silence of the Lambs*?
2. **Anagram** – The anagram is always an author's name: ALIAS FUN BASKETS
3. **Book Quote** – Can you name the book from which this quote comes? 'I know not all that may be coming, but be it what it will, I'll go to it laughing.' Is that from: A) *The Diary of a Nobody* by George and Weedon Grossmith, B) *Diary of a Madman* by Nikolay Gogol, C) *Moby Dick* by Herman Melville or D) *Must the Show Go On?* by Les Dennis
4. T'Pau's 1987 monster hit 'China in Your Hand' was inspired by which classic novel from 1818?
5. **Odd One Out** – Which of the following is not a real James Herriot title: A) *It Shouldn't Happen to a Vet*, B) *Let Sleeping Vets Lie*, C) *The Vixen and the Vet* or D) *Vets Might Fly*?
6. **Poetry Corner** – What is the next line? This quiz the poem is 'Macavity – the Mystery Cat' by T. S. Eliot: 'Macavity's a Mystery Cat: he's called the Hidden Paw . . .'
7. **Fact or Fiction** – Which of the following is a fact about Salman Rushdie: A) at Cambridge University Salman

Rushdie was in a progressive rock band called the Magic Bus Conductors, B) Salman Rushdie loves *Emmerdale* and once appeared as an extra in the Woolpack or C) Salman Rushdie once worked in advertising and came up with the fresh-cream cake campaign 'Naughty, but nice'?

8. This science-fiction book from 1896 has been adapted for film many times. The first version was a silent French film in 1913. There is a 1977 version starring Burt Lancaster and an extremely troubled production was released in 1996 starring Marlon Brando. Tim Burton made a version when he was just thirteen and the American art-rock band Devo took inspiration from the book for their first album title, *Q:Are we not men? A: No we are Devo!* Can you name the book?

9. **What Year?** – In which year did these literary events take place? If you're playing in teams give a point to whichever team gets nearest. Published this year are Martin Amis's *The Rachel Papers*, J. G. Ballard's *Crash* and Raymond Briggs's *Father Christmas*. Penelope Lively wins the Carnegie Medal for *The Ghost of Thomas Kempe*. Virago Press is founded by Carmen Callil to publish classics by female authors. J. R .R. Tolkien, Noël Coward and W. H. Auden all pass away. Stephenie Meyer, Frances Hardinge and Victoria Coren Mitchell are all born.

10. **Give Me Five** – Eric Carle's *The Very Hungry Caterpillar* is a children's classic but can you remember what it ate? There are sixteen items of food. Name five for 5 points.

**Round 2, Part A) RomeNo or JuliYes** – Are these genuine Shakespeare insults or made up by me? A point for each correctly identified insult. If you think it's genuine write or say JuliYes! If you think it's made up then it's RomeNo!

11. That swollen parcel of dropsies
12. Son of a banker's hand
13. A fusty nut with no kernel
14. Thou cream-faced loon
15. Rancid pool of dog spittle

**Round 2, Part B) Blankety Books** – Find the missing word: there's always a theme and this quiz the theme is . . . temperature. A point for each one you get:

16. *In the [Blank] of the Night* by John Ball
17. *[Blank] a Frog* by Christopher Brookmyre
18. *Love in a [Blank] Climate* by Nancy Mitford
19. *[Blank] Hand Luke* by Donn Pearce
20. *[Blank] Milk* by Deborah Levy

**Round 3, Part A) Two of a Kind** – I will describe a character and then an author. They share the same initials so if you know one it will help you get the other. A point for each you can name:

21. Character: The anti-hero created by Patricia Highsmith who appeared in five novels between 1955 and 1991; he has been played on film by Alain Delon and Matt Damon. Author: The children's author and illustrator who is best known for illustrating the 'Horrid Henry' series, David Walliams's books and his own 'Little Princess' series.
22. Character: The character is a middle-aged literary scholar who pursues Lolita in Nabokov's 1955 novel, played in Stanley Kubrick's film by James Mason. Author: A German-born poet, novelist and painter; his best-known works include *Steppenwolf* and *Siddhartha*; he was awarded the Nobel Prize in Literature in 1946.

23. Character: The teenage protagonist of J. D. Salinger's 1951 novel *The Catcher in the Rye*. Author: The bestselling American thriller writer known for the 'Myron Bolitar' series and whose 2015 novel *The Stranger* was made into a Netflix series in 2020.

24. Character: The titular diarist created by Helen Fielding who first appeared in a column in the *Independent* in 1995, followed by a novel in 1996; she has been played three times on screen by Renée Zellweger. Author: The English author best known for his 'Redwall' series of fantasy novels for children that began in 1986 and ended in 2011 with the posthumously published *Rogue Crew*.

25. Character: And finally, this character is the male protagonist of George Orwell's *1984*. Author: The author of many science-fiction novels but who is better known as an actor and whose first non-fiction book is called *Captain's Log*.

**Round 3, Part B) Partners** – Fill in the missing partner for 1 point and name the author for another point:

26. *The Sound and the* what?, 1929
27. *Daisy Jones and the* what?, 2019
28. *The Spy and the* what?, 2018
29. *The Heart and the* what?, 2010
30. *The Beautiful and the* what?, 1922

**Round 4, Part A) Also an Author** – More famous for other things, who are these published authors? A point for each:

31. This man is better known as a TV gardener, but he has also written ten novels, including *The Last Lighthouse*

*Keeper* and *Mr MacGregor*, some of his books are quite racy.

32. Better known as an actor, this Hollywood star also directs, and in 2018 his first novel *Bob Honey Who Just Do Stuff* was published; at the time he claimed being a writer would 'dominate my creative energies for the foreseeable future' and indeed the sequel *Bob Honey Sings Jimmy Crack Corn* was published in 2019.

33. This Canadian was better known for being a singer-songwriter and a poet, but he wrote two novels, *The Favourite Game* in 1963 and *Beautiful Losers* in 1966, before finding fame with his first LP in 1967.

34. Better known as a dancer, this *Strictly Come Dancing* star released his debut novel *One Enchanted Evening* in 2018.

35. This comedy actor and writer is best known for being a member of the Monty Python team, but he has had two novels published, *Hemingway's Chair* in 1995 and *The Truth* in 2012.

**Round 4, Part B) Literature Links and Lists** – Answer these novel conundrums for a point each:

36. What word ends these books: David Baddiel's *The Parent* …, Douglas Adams's *Dirk Gently's Holistic Detective* …' and Alexander McCall Smith's *The No. 1 Ladies' Detective* …?

37. What links the short story by Edgar Allan Poe from 1843 (Lisa Simpson creates a diorama of a scene from it in the classic *Simpsons* episode 'Lisa's Rival'), Chuck Palahniuk's novel where the first rule is you can't talk about it, Dashiell Hammett's fictional detective in *The Maltese Falcon* and the fourth James Bond novel by Ian Fleming?

38. What's next in this list: *Origin, Inferno, The Lost Symbol, The Da Vinci Code* ...?
39. What links Vladimir Nabokov, David Sedaris and Noam Chomsky: A) they share a birth date, B) they have all been shot or C) they all have insects named after them?
40. What occupation features in the titles of books by Dorothy L. Sayers, Beatrix Potter and two books by John le Carré?

Finally, there are six 'SayWhatYouSee' visual representations of novels. Give yourself a point for the author and a point for the title.

Total up your answers and see how many you scored.
   The highest score possible on this quiz is 66.
   Thanks for playing!

# The Answers

1. B) *Red Dragon*, 1981 (*The Silence of the Lambs*, 1988, *Hannibal*, 1999)
2. Sebastian Faulks
3. C) *Moby Dick* by Herman Melville
4. *Frankenstein*
5. C) *The Vixen and the Vet* (a book by Katie Regnery, the first in the 'A Modern Fairytale' series)
6. 'For he's the master criminal who can defy the Law'
7. C) He worked in advertising and came up with the 'Naughty but nice' line\*
8. *The Island of Doctor Moreau* by H. G. Wells†
9. 1973‡
10. Apple, pears, plums, strawberries, oranges, chocolate cake, ice-cream cone, pickle, Swiss cheese, salami, lollipop, cherry pie, sausage, cupcake, watermelon, one green leaf
11. JuliYes! It's from *Henry IV*
12. RomeNo!

\* He also came up with 'Irresistibubble' for Aero chocolate bars and 'That'll do nicely' for American Express.

† The version with Brando has to be seen to be believed – he seems to be channelling late British actor Derek Nimmo; a documentary (*Lost Soul: The Doomed Journey of Richard Stanley's Island of Dr Moreau*) about the making of this version is a fascinating watch.

‡ One way to remember that Tolkien died in 1973 is to think of the number of rings in *The Lord of the Rings*, i.e. 1 Ring to Rule Them All; 9 Rings for Men; 7 for Dwarves; 3 for the Elves.

13. JuliYes! It's from *Troilus and Cressida*
14. JuliYes! It's from *Macbeth*
15. RomeNo!
16. *Heat*
17. *Boiling*
18. *Cold*
20. *Cool*
20. *Hot*
21. Tom Ripley and Tony Ross
22. Humbert Humbert and Hermann Hesse
23. Holden Caulfield and Harlan Coben
24. Bridget Jones and Brian Jacques
25. Winston Smith and William Shatner
26. *The Sound and the Fury* by William Faulkner
27. *Daisy Jones and the Six* by Taylor Jenkins Reid
28. *The Spy and the Traitor* by Ben Macintyre
29. *The Heart and the Bottle* by Oliver Jeffers
30. *The Beautiful and the Damned* by F. Scott Fitzgerald
31. Alan Titchmarsh*
32. Sean Penn†
33. Leonard Cohen
34. Anton Du Beke
35. Michael Palin
36. *Agency*
37. Suits in playing cards: Edgar Allan Poe's *The Tell Tale Heart*, Chuck Palahniuk's *Fight **Club***, Dashiell Hammett's 'Sam **Spade**' and Ian Fleming's ***Diamonds*** *are Forever*

---

* Alan Titchmarsh came second to Sebastian Faulks in the 2004 Bad Sex Awards.
† Penn's book got some stinging reviews; the headline of the *Guardian*'s review was 'Sean Penn's debut novel – repellent and stupid on so many levels', and Mark Hill on Cracked.com called it 'the worst novel in human history'.

38. *Angels & Demons*: these are Dan Brown's Robert Langdon series in reverse published order
39. C) They all have insects named after them*
40. Tailor: *The Nine Tailors* by Dorothy L. Sayers, *The Tailor of Gloucester* by Beatrix Potter, *Tinker Tailor Soldier Spy* and *The Tailor of Panama* by John le Carré
41. *I Capture the Castle* by Dodie Smith
42. *The Girl Who Kicked the Hornet's Nest* by Steig Larsson
43. *The Name of the Rose* by Umberto Eco
44. *The Day of the Locust* by Nathanael West
45. *Notes from the Underground* by Fyodor Doestoevsky
46. *The Song of Achilles* by Madeline Miller

* Nabokov has a butterfly called 'Nabokovia' named after him (he loved butterflies and moths and studied them all his life); Sedaris has a beetle named after him and Chomsky a bee.

# Quiz Number 8

**Round 1: This and That** . . . all the questions in this round are worth 1 point except question 10, which is worth 5.

1. **The First Question** – Which of these books was published first: A) *The Sea Inside* by Philip Hoare, B) *The Sea* by John Banville or C) *The Sea, the Sea* by Iris Murdoch?

2. **Anagram** – The anagram is always an author's name: CARNAGE LATER

3. **Book Quote** – Can you name the book from which this quote comes? 'Life isn't all beer and skittles; but beer and skittles, or something better of the same sort, must form a good part of every Englishman's education.' Is it from: A) *Lucky Jim* by Kingsley Amis, B) *Tom Brown's Schooldays* by Thomas Hughes, C) *Our Man in Havana* by Graham Greene or D) *And Another Thing* by Jeremy Clarkson?

4. Which Richard Adams novel features the language Lapine?

5. **Odd One Out** – Which of the following is not a real book by P.G. Wodehouse: A) *Stiff Upper Lip, Jeeves*, B) *Right Ho, Jeeves*, C) *Broadway, Jeeves?* or D) *Jeeves and the Feudal Spirit*?

6. **Poetry Corner** – What is the next line? This quiz the poem is 'She Walks in Beauty' by George Gordon, Lord Byron: 'She walks in beauty, like the night . . .'

7. **Fact or Fiction** – Which of the following is a fact about Julia Donaldson: A) Julia Donaldson is now famous as

a children's author but her first published book was a *Reader's Digest* cookery book called *Cooking with Children* published in 1975, B) Julia, alongside her husband Malcolm, was involved in the British folk music scene and even released an LP in 1977 or C) before taking up writing full time, Julia Donaldson worked for Radio 4 and came up with the format for *Just a Minute*, which is still running today?

8. Which book from 1611 is not out of copyright in Britain — because the rights are held in perpetuity by the British Crown?

9. **What Year?** – In which year did these literary events take place? If you're playing in teams give a point to whichever team gets nearest. Salman Rushdie's *Midnight's Children* wins the 'best of the Bookers'. New books published this year include *Breaking Dawn* by Stephenie Meyer, *Paper Towns* by John Green and Eleanor Catton's debut *The Rehearsal*, and David Foster Wallace and Harold Pinter both pass away.

10. **Give Me Five** – There are seven books that make up C. S. Lewis's 'Chronicles of Narnia'. Name five of them for 5 points.

**Round 2, Part A) Ho Ho Ho!** – Comedians and literature. Each question is worth 1 point:

11. Whose autobiographical books include *Hitler: My Part in His Downfall*, *Monty: His Part in My Victory* and *Mussolini: His Part in My Downfall*?

12. Which member of the legendary Marx Brothers wrote *Memoirs of a Mangy Lover*, published in 1963?

13. Which stand-up comedian has published the novels *Bullet Points*, *The Knot* and *The Place That Didn't Exist*?

14. Which comedian wrote about fifty male historical figures in *A Load of Old Balls* (1994)? She also wrote a sequel about women called *A Load of Ball Crunchers* (1996) and more recently released *Born Lippy: How to do Female*.

15. True or false: Les Dawson had a romance novel published under the name Leslie de Sondaw.

**Round 2, Part B) Blankety Books** – Find the missing word: there's always a theme and this quiz the theme is . . . chemical elements. A point for each one you get:

16. *The [Blank] Man* by Ted Hughes
17. *The [Blank] Linings Playbook* by Matthew Quick
18. *The [Blank] Bible* by John Kennedy Toole
19. *He Kills [Blanks]* by Jake Arnott
20. *Rancid [Blank]* by James Hawes

**Round 3, Part A) Two of a Kind** – I will describe a character and then an author. They share the same initials so if you know one it will help you get the other. A point for each you can name:

21. Character: The Shakespeare character that falls in love with Romeo. Author: The Scottish author probably best known for writing romantic comedies, including the 'Beach Street Bakery' and the 'Cupcake Café' books; she also writes science fiction including 2015's *Resistance Is Futile*.

22. Character: Created by Jacqueline Wilson in 1991, this character went on to appear in her own CBBC TV series, and the series of books that featured her was the most borrowed from UK libraries between 2000 and 2010. Author: American fantasy-fiction author of the

'Shannara' series, he has sold over 21 million copies of his books.

23. Character: The lead male protagonist of Margaret Mitchell's novel *Gone with the Wind*, he was played in the film version by Clark Gable. Author: The writer and illustrator of *Fungus the Bogeyman*, *When the Wind Blows* and, most famously, *The Snowman*.

24. Character: Created by Elmore Leonard, a loan shark who becomes involved in the movie business first in the 1990 novel *Get Shorty* and then in the sequel *Be Cool*; he was played in the films by John Travolta. Author: Best known for his first novel *Fight Club*, others include *Choke* and *Rant*.

25. Character: And finally, the young lad in Barry Hine's classic Yorkshire-set novel *A Kestrel for a Knave*; the book was filmed by Ken Loach and re-titled *Kes*. Author: The bestselling author of the hugely successful 'Sharpe' series of books set in the Napoleonic wars; Sharpe was played in the long-running TV series by Sean Bean.

**Round 3, Part B) Whodunit? Or rather Whosolvedit?**
– Link the cases to the detectives for a point:

26. *The Murder of Roger Ackroyd*
27. *The Monster in the Box*
28. 'The Red-Headed League'
29. *The Killings at Badger's Drift*
30. *The Madman of Bergerac*

**Round 4, Part A) Tales of the Cities** – I will give you the city in which the book is set, the author's initials and year of release. Just tell me the book's title for 1 point:

31. Moscow, MB, 1966
32. Dublin, JJ, 1922
33. Edinburgh, MS, 1961
34. San Francisco, VS, 1986
35. Paris, VH, 1862

**Round 4, Part B) Literature Links and Lists** – Answer these novel conundrums for a point each:

36. What name features in the titles of books by Henry Fielding, Thomas Hughes and Michelle Magorian?
37. What comes next in this list: *The Kalahari Typing School for Men*, *Morality for Beautiful Girls*, *Tears of the Giraffe* . . .?
38. Who could be next in this list: Alan Bennett, Charles Dickens, E. M. Forster . . .?
39. What links the books *Savrola* from 1900, *The Devil's Tune* from 2003 and *Open Arms* from 2017?
40. What kind of establishment features in the title of books by John Irving, Anita Brookner and Arthur Hailey?

Finally, there are six 'SayWhatYouSee' visual representations of novels. Give yourself a point for the author and a point for the title.

Total up your answers and see how many you scored.
   The highest score possible on this quiz is 61.
   Thanks for playing!

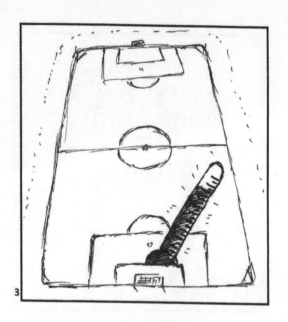

1903 – 1984

# The Answers

1. A) *The Sea, the Sea*, 1978 (*The Sea Inside*, 2013, *The Sea*, 2005)
2. Angela Carter
3. B) *Tom Brown's Schooldays* by Thomas Hughes
4. *Watership Down*
5. C) *Broadway, Jeeves?* (this is a book by the actor Martin Jarvis)
6. 'Of cloudless climes and starry skies'
7. B) Julia Donaldson and her husband released an album called *First 14*, which you can still buy on her website
8. The King James Bible (the copyright is covered by a Royal Prerogative)
9. 2008
10. In publication order: *The Lion the Witch and the Wardrobe*, *Prince Caspian*, *The Voyage of the Dawn Treader*, *The Silver Chair*, *The Horse and His Boy*, *The Magician's Nephew*, *The Last Battle*
11. Spike Milligan
12. Groucho Marx*
13. Mark Watson
14. Jo Brand

* Groucho, of course, is famous for the quote 'Outside of a dog, a book is a man's best friend. Inside of a dog it's too dark to read.' Harpo also released an autobiography (written with Roland Barber) called *Harpo Speaks!* in 1961.

15. False*
16. *Iron*
17. *Silver*
18. *Neon*
19. *Coppers*
20. *Aluminium*
21. Juliet Capulet and Jenny Colgan
22. Tracy Beaker and Terry Brooks
23. Rhett Butler and Raymond Briggs
24. Chili Palmer and Chuck Palahniuk
25. Billy Casper and Bernard Cornwell OBE†
26. Hercule Poirot – Agatha Christie
27. Inspector Wexford – Ruth Rendell
28. Sherlock Holmes – Arthur Conan Doyle
29. Inspector John Barnaby – Caroline Graham
30. Inspector Maigret – Georges Simenon‡
31. *The Master and Margarita* by Mikhail Bulgakov

* Les Dawson did write a romance novel called 'An Echo of Shadows' under the nom de plume Maria Brett-Cooper, but it was never published.

† In the books Sharpe was originally from the south, with black hair, but Bernard Cornwell was so taken with Sean Bean's performance (with blond hair and very much from the north) he not only stopped mentioning Sharpe's hair colour, but (in books published after the show began) also invented a back story whereby he moved to Yorkshire at age fifteen – just to explain Bean's accent.

‡ Not Jim Bergerac, that would have been two appearances in a row for John Nettles! There are some *Bergerac* books, written after the show by Andrew Saville. And if you're a big fan there is *Bergerac's Jersey* by Nettles himself. Also, if you have ever wondered why Nettles's character in *Midsomer Murders* was replaced by his cousin, it's because the show is known as *Inspector Barnaby* in overseas territories – and is very popular.

32. *Ulysses* by James Joyce
33. *The Prime of Miss Jean Brodie* by Muriel Spark
34. *The Golden Gate* by Vikram Seth
35. *Les Misérables* by Victor Hugo
36. Tom: *Tom Jones* by Henry Fielding, *Tom Brown's Schooldays* by Thomas Hughes, *Goodnight Mr Tom* by Michelle Magorian
37. *The No. 1 Ladies' Detective Agency*: these are books in the Alexander McCall Smith series from four to one
38. Georgette Heyer or Gill Hornby or any other author with the initials G. H. (A. B. – C. D. – E. F. – G. H.)
39. They are all fiction written by politicians: Winston Churchill, *Savrola*, Iain Duncan Smith, *The Devil's Tune*, Vince Cable, *Open Arms*
40. A hotel: *Hotel New Hampshire* by John Irving, *Hotel du Lac* by Anita Brookner, *Hotel* by Arthur Hailey
41. *Northern Lights* by Philip Pullman
42. *The Constant Gardner* by John Le Carre
43. *Fever Pitch* by Nick Hornby
44. *Life of Pi* by Yann Martel
45. *Revolutionary Road* by Richard Yates
46. *The Essex Serpent* by Sarah Perry

# Quiz Number 9

**Round 1: This and That . . .** all the questions in this round are worth 1 point except question 10, which is worth 5.

1. **The First Question** – Which of these sci-fi classics was published first: A) *When Worlds Collide* by Edwin Balmer and Philip Wylie, B) *The War of the Worlds* by H. G. Wells or C) *Brave New World* by Aldous Huxley?

2. **Anagram** – The anagram is always an author's name: THAT HIP IRISH MAGIC

3. **Book Quote** – Can you name the book from which this quote comes? 'I would always rather be happy than dignified.' Is it from: A) *The Catcher in the Rye* by J. D. Salinger, B) *Winnie the Pooh* by A. A. Milne, C) *Jane Eyre* by Charlotte Brontë or D) *Me Me Me* by Charlotte Crosby?

4. Since 1981 'Sloppy Joe's' restaurant and bar in Key West, Florida, has held an annual lookalike convention as part of the celebrations to remember which famous American author?

5. **Odd One Out** – Which of the following is not a real James Patterson novel: A) *Along Came a Spider*, B) *Mary, Mary*, C) *Hickory Dickory Dock* or D) *Four Blind Mice*?

6. **Poetry Corner** – What is the next line? This quiz the poem is 'Sonnet 18: Shall I compare thee to a summer's day?' by William Shakespeare: 'Shall I compare thee to a summer's day? . . .'

7. **Fact or Fiction** – Which of the following is a fact about Martina Cole: A) in 2010 she launched a record

company called Hostage Music, B) in 2008 she presented a documentary on ITV3 called *Martina Coles' Moles* about industrial spies or C) she is the daughter of *Minder* actor George Cole?

8. This 1864 sci-fi classic has been adapted many times: in 1959 a popular film was released starring James Mason; in 2008 there was another hit film this time starring Brendan Fraser, though this was actually a sequel to the book. There have been many TV and radio versions, computer and board games, even theme-park rides. In 1974 Rick Wakeman had a no. 1 with a concept album based on this book; he then followed that twenty-five years later with a sequel. Can you name the book?

9. **What Year?** – In which year did these literary events take place? If you're playing in teams give a point to whichever team gets nearest. Published this year: *Howards End* by E. M. Forster and *The Secret Garden* by Frances Hodgson Burnett. The signing of the Buenos Aries Convention marks the first international recognition of copyright. Leo Tolstoy dies, as does Mark Twain.

10. **Give Me Five** – The titles of a total of nine Man Booker Prize winners (up to 2019) start with 'The' and have three words in the title. Name five titles for 5 points.

**Round 2, Part A) Carroll on Regardless** – Were these words invented by Lewis Carroll or not? A point for every one you get right:

11. Nightmare
12. Chortle
13. Groggy
14. Mimsy
15. Snark

**Round 2, Part B) Blankety Books** – Find the missing word: there's always a theme and this quiz the theme is . . . one-word names of bands or singers. A point for each one you get:

16. *[Blank] Me Deadly* by Mickey Spillane
17. *The [Blank] of the Damned* by Anne Rice
18. *Mr Cleghorn's [Blank]* by Judith Kerr
19. *Angel [Blank]* by J. B. Priestley
20. *According to [Blank]* by Dawn French

**Round 3, Part A) Two of a Kind** – I will describe a character and then an author. They share the same initials so if you know one it will help you get the other. A point for each you can name:

21. Character: Created by Daniel Defoe in 1719, this character spends twenty-eight years on a remote desert island. Author: The American crime author of such classics as *Farewell My Lovely* and *The Long Goodbye*
22. Character: This character is a detective and psychologist based in Washington, DC, and created by James Patterson; he has been played in two films by Morgan Freeman. Author: The French-Algerian philosopher, author and journalist who won the Nobel Prize in Literature in 1957; his novels include *The Stranger*, *The Plague* and *The Fall*.
23. Character: The main protagonist of Mario Puzo's *The Godfather*, the son of Vito – played in the films by Al Pacino. Author: The Pulitzer Prize-winning author of *The Amazing Adventures of Kavalier and Clay*, *Wonder Boys* and *Moonglow*; in 2019 he became show runner on the new *Star Trek* 'Picard' series.

24. Character: The A & R man and amoral swine at the heart of John Niven's 2008 book *Kill Your Friends*, played in the film by Nicholas Hoult. Author: The American author, cartoonist, playwright and songwriter (he wrote 'A Boy Named Sue') who wrote many children's books, was translated into 30 languages and sold over 20 million copies before his death in 1999.

25. Character: And finally, from George R. R. Martin's 'A Song of Ice and Fire' series of books, this character first appeared in *A Game of Thrones*; she is the daughter of King Aerys II; one of the last survivors of her house, she trains three dragons to aid her; she's played in the TV series by Emilia Clarke. Author: The Pulitzer Prize-winning author of *The Goldfinch*, *Secret History* and *The Little Friend*.

**Round 3, Part B) Siblings** – Name the book from the siblings for a point, and the author for another. I will also give you the year the book was published:

26. Marianne and Elinor Dashwood, 1811
27. Rahel and Estha (short for Esthappen), 1997
28. Lucy and Freddy Honeychurch, 1908
29. Cecilia, Lux, Bonnie, Mary and Therese Lisbon, 1993
30. Maggie and Tom Tulliver, 1860

**Round 4, Part A) Mr Who?** – Roger Hargreaves's Mr Men series is popular all over the world but can you identify these characters from their translated names?

31. Who in Norway is called 'Herr Dumpidump'?
32. In Portugal he is known as 'Senor Tonto' but in English?
33. In France he's called 'Monsieur Bing' but what is the English translation?

34. In Denmark they call him 'Faetter Dumbum'; what do the English call him?

35. And ending in Norway, we have 'Herr Atscho', otherwise known as . . .?

**Round 4, Part B) Literature Links and Lists** – Answer these novel conundrums for a point each.

36. What comes next in this list: *A Darkling Plain, Infernal Devices, Predator's Gold* and then?

37. What character links these books by Sophie Hannah: *The Killings at Kingfisher Hill, The Monogram Murders* and *Closed Casket*?

38. What links 'Mirth', 'Sleep', 'Silk' and 'the Dead'?

39. What occupation connects Mildred Ratched from *One Flew over the Cuckoo's Nest*, Hana from *The English Patient* and Catherine Barkley from *A Farewell to Arms*?

40. In which country were these authors born: Knut Hamsun, Jostein Gaarder and Karl Ove Knausgård?

Finally, there are six 'SayWhatYouSee' visual representations of novels. Give yourself a point for the author and a point for the title.

Total up your answers and see how many you scored.

The highest score possible on this quiz is 66.

Thanks for playing!

# The Answers

1. B) *The War of the Worlds*, 1898 (*When Worlds Collide*, 1933, *Brave New World*, 1932)
2. Patricia Highsmith
3. *Jane Eyre* by Charlotte Brontë
4. Ernest Hemingway*
5. C) *Hickory Dickory Dock* (this is an Agatha Christie novel)
6. 'Thou art more lovely and more temperate'
7. A) She launched a record label†
8. *Journey to the Centre of the Earth* by Jules Verne
9. 1910‡
10. Bernice Rubens, *The Elected Member*; Keri Hulme, *The Bone People*; Kingsley Amis, *The Old Devils*; Ben Okri, *The Famished Road*; Michael Ondaatje, *The English*

---

* In 2019 Joe Maxey beat 141 other Hemingway lookalikes to the crown.

† Martina Cole did this as she loved the theme tune to *The Sopranos* TV show ('Woke Up This Morning') by Alabama 3 and wanted to sign them. She did make a TV series (about female serial killers, not spies) and featured their song 'Too Sick to Pray'.

‡ Halley's Comet passed close to Earth this year and in 1909 Twain said, 'I came in with Halley's comet in 1835. It's coming again next year [1910], and I expect to go out with it. The Almighty has said no doubt, "Now here are these two unaccountable freaks; they came in together, they must go out together."'

*Patient*; Pat Barker, *The Ghost Road*; Margaret Atwood, *The Blind Assassin*; Aravind Adiga, *The White Tiger*; Howard Jacobson, *The Finkler Question*

11. No*

12. Yes (Carroll coined the word as a blend of chuckle and snort in 1871 in *Alice Through the Looking Glass*)

13. No†

14. Yes (coined by Lewis Carroll in 1855 as a blend of miserable and flimsy)

15. Yes (coined by Carroll in 1876 in his poem, *The Hunting of the Snark*)

16. *Kiss*

17. *Queen*

18. *Seal*

19. *Pavement*

20. *Yes*

21. Robinson Crusoe and Raymond Chandler‡

22. Alex Cross and Albert Camus§

---

* It sounds as though it refers to a female horse, but in fact the 'mare' part of the word 'nightmare' (a terrifying dream) comes from Germanic folklore, in which a 'mare' is an evil female spirit or goblin that sits upon a sleeper's chest.

† It originated in the eighteenth century with a British man named Admiral Vernon, whose sailors gave him the nickname 'Old Grog' on account of his cloak, which was made from a material called 'grogram', a weatherproof mixture of silk and wool. In 1740, he decreed that his sailors should be served their rum diluted with water, rather than neat. This was called 'grog', and the feeling experienced by sailors when they had drunk too much of it was thus called 'groggy'.

‡ Raymond Chandler only began writing aged forty-four after losing his job as an oil company executive in the Great Depression.

§ Albert Camus loved football and was an excellent goalkeeper.

23. Michael Corleone and Michael Chabon
24. Steven Stelfox and Shel Silverstein
25. Daenerys Targaryen and Donna Tartt
26. *Sense and Sensibility* by Jane Austen
27. *The God of Small Things* by Arundhati Roy
28. *A Room with a View* by E. M. Forster
29. *The Virgin Suicides* by Jeffrey Eugenides
30. *The Mill on the Floss* by George Eliot
31. Mr Bump
32. Mr Silly
33. Mr Bounce
34. Mr Dizzy
35. Mr Sneeze
36. *Mortal Engines*: these are the Philip Reeve's 'Mortal Engines' quartet in reverse publication order
37. Hercule Poirot: they are all new Poirot mysteries
38. They are all *The House of . . .* novels: *The House of Mirth* by Edith Wharton, *The House of Sleep* by Jonathan Coe, *The House of Silk* by Anthony Horowitz, *The House of the Dead* by Fyodor Dostoevsky
39. They are all nurses
40. Norway
41. *Bleak House* by Charles Dickens
42. *Firestarter* by Stephen King
43. *The Cuckoo's Calling* by Robert Galbraith
44. *Microserfs* by Douglas Coupland
45. *The Cider House Rules* by John Irving
46. *Runaway Horses* by Yukio Mishima

# Quiz Number 10

**Round 1: This and That . . .** all the questions in this round are worth 1 point except question 10, which is worth 5.

1. **The First Question** – Which of these famous literary Alans was born first: A) Alan Hollinghurst, B) Alan Moore or C) Alan Bennett?
2. **Anagram** – The anagram is always an author's name: GIN IN FLAME
3. **Book Quote** – Can you name the book from which this quote comes? 'Beware; for I am fearless and therefore powerful.' Is it from: A) *I Am Legend* by Richard Matheson, B) *It* by Stephen King, C) *Frankenstein* by Mary Shelley or D) *The Path to Power* by Margaret Thatcher?
4. About which otter did Henry Williamson write a 1927 novel?
5. **Odd One Out** – Which of the following is not a real John Grisham title: A) *The Client*, B) *The Crown Court*, C) *The Summons* or D) *The Appeal*?
6. **Poetry Corner** – What is the next line? This quiz the poem is 'The Raven' by Edgar Allan Poe: 'Once upon a midnight dreary . . .'
7. **Fact or Fiction** – Which of the following is a fact about Stephen King: A) despite being the master of horror, King is terrified of spiders and will not enter a hotel room until his PA has checked it, B) one of his first writing credits was on the original *Twilight Zone* series; his

one episode was called 'The Doomsday Machine', or C) he collaborated on a musical with American singer John Mellencamp called *Ghost Brothers of Darkland County*?

8. Which famous actor released the autobiography *The Elephant to Hollywood*?

9. **What Year?** – In which year did these literary events take place? If you're playing in teams give a point to whichever team gets nearest. Published this year: Dan Brown's *The Lost Symbol*, Thomas Pynchon's *Inherent Vice* and Jacqueline Wilson's *Hetty Feather*. Hilary Mantel wins the Booker for *Wolf Hall*. Frank McCourt and John Updike both pass away and three films based on books are in the top 10 box office hits of the year: *Angels and Demons* at 9, *New Moon* at 7 and *Harry Potter and the Half-Blood Prince* at 2.

10. **Give Me Five** – Name the five locations (four countries and one island) in the titles of the classic 'Asterix' series by Goscinny and Uderzo (up to 1979). A point for each correct location.

**Round 2, Part A) There is a Place in Hull for Me and My Friends** – Are these Morrissey lyrics or Philip Larkin quotes? A point for each you identify correctly:

11. 'I have no enemies, but my friends don't like me'
12. 'I praise the day that brings you pain, QCs obsessed with sleaze, Frantic for Fame'
13. 'So sleep and dream of love, because it's the closest you will get to love'
14. 'The slums, the canal, the churches ornate and mad, In the evening sun. It is intensely sad'
15. 'Man hands on misery to man. It deepens like a coastal shelf. Get out as early as you can, And don't have any kids yourself'

**Round 2, Part B) Blankety Books** – Find the missing word: there's always a theme and this quiz the theme is . . . relations. A point for each one you get:

16. *Wolf [Blank]* by Michelle Paver
17. *My [Blank] Rachel* by Daphne du Maurier
18. *Travels with My [Blank]* by Graham Greene
19. *The Good [Blank]* by Karin Slaughter
20. *[Blank] Night* by Kurt Vonnegut

**Round 3, Part A) Two of a Kind** – I will describe a character and then an author and they share the same initials. So, if you know one it will help you get the other. A point for each you can name.

21. Character: The central male vampire from Stephenie Meyer's 'Twilight' series who falls in love and marries Bella Swan. Author: The American writer and illustrator best known for *The Very Hungry Caterpillar*.

22. Character: Arthur Conan Doyle's famous detective who lives at 221B Baker Street, London; his cases are narrated by his friend and biographer Dr John Watson; he first appeared in 1887 in *A Study in Scarlet*. Author: The British author whose 2006 book *Little Face*, the first in the 'Zailer and Waterhouse' series, was a huge success; she has since added another nine books to this series and written new 'Hercule Poirot' novels, the first being *The Monogram Murders* in 2014.

23. Character: Created by Thomas Harris, she first appears in *The Silence of the Lambs* where she attempts to enlist Hannibal Lector's assistance in catching the serial killer Buffalo Bill. Author: The American novelist of *American Wife*, *Prep*, *Eligible* and *Sisterland*.

24. Character: Created by E. B. White in 1945, he is a 2-inch tall talking mouse; he was voiced in the films by Michael J Fox. Author: The Swedish journalist and writer best known for creating the 'Millennium Trilogy', featuring Lisbeth Salander; he sadly passed away in 2004 at the age of just fifty.

25. Character: The character from Kafka's *Metamorphosis* who awakes one morning to find he has transformed into a giant insect. Author: The Belgian author, born in 1903, best known for his series of detective novels featuring Inspector Maigret.

**Round 3, Part B) Which Brontë?** – Simply that: which Brontë sister wrote the below titles: Emily, Anne or Charlotte? A point for each correct answer:

26. *The Tenant of Wildfell Hall*
27. *Villette*
28. *Shirley*
29. *Agnes Grey*
30. *Wuthering Heights*

**Round 4, Part A) Tomes of Terror** – Questions about horror books, each worth a putrefying point:

31. Richard Bachman is a penname for which famous horror writer?
32. In the Helen Nicoll children's books, what are the names of the witch and her cat? (Half a point each)
33. Netflix had a big hit with its 2018 adaptation of the 1959 novel *The Haunting of Hill House* – can you name the American-born author?
34. Which *Peanuts* character sits in the Pumpkin Patch every year awaiting the arrival of 'The Great Pumpkin'?

35. Which member of TV and radio comedy team the League of Gentlemen wrote *The Haunted Book*?

**Round 4, Part B) Literature Links and Lists** – Answer these novel conundrums for a point each:

36. What type of building connects books by Dodie Smith, Diana Wynne Jones and Shirley Jackson?
37. What comes next: *The Cuckoo's Calling*, *The Silkworm*, *Career of Evil*?
38. What links Douglas Adams, George Eliot and Christina Rossetti?
39. Name the final book in this trilogy by Pat Barker: *Regeneration*, *The Eye in the Door* and . . .?
40. What word appears in the title of books by Max Porter, Jacqueline Wilson and A. E. W. Mason?

Finally, there are six 'SayWhatYouSee' visual representations of novels. Give yourself a point for the author and a point for the title.

Total up your answers and see how many you scored.
    The highest score possible on this quiz is 61.
    Thanks for playing!

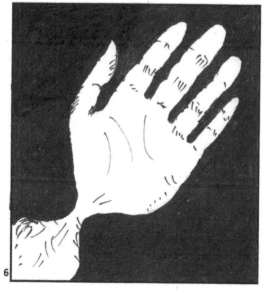

# The Answers

1. C) Alan Bennett, 1934 (Alan Hollinghurst, 1964, Alan Moore, 1953)
2. Ian Fleming
3. C) *Frankenstein* by Mary Shelley
4. Tarka
5. B) *The Crown Court* (Grisham is an American author and writes predominantly about the USA)
6. 'While I pondered, weak and weary'
7. C) King and Mellencamp collaborated in 2012
8. Michael Caine*
9. 2009
10. Britain, Corsica, Spain. Switzerland and Belgium; you can have a point for 'Gaul' too – the first book is called *Asterix the Gaul* and Gaul was the name of France and a surrounding area during the Iron Age
11. Larkin (said to a friend)
12. Morrissey, 'Sorrow Will Come in the End'
13. Morrissey, 'November Spawned a Monster'
14. Larkin, 'Money'
15. Larkin, 'This Be the Verse'
16. *Brother*
17. *Cousin*
18. *Aunt*
19. *Daughter*
20. *Mother*

* The 'Elephant' being the Elephant & Castle area of London where Caine grew up.

21. Edward Cullen and Eric Carle
22. Sherlock Holmes and Sophie Hannah
23. Clarice Starling and Curtis Sittenfeld
24. Stuart Little and Stieg Larsson*
25. Gregor Samsa and Georges Simenon
26. Anne
27. Charlotte
28. Charlotte
29. Anne
30. Emily
31. Stephen King
32. Meg and Mog
33. Shirley Jackson
34. Linus van Pelt†
35. Jeremy Dyson‡
36. Castle: Dodie Smith's *I Capture the Castle*, Diana Wynne Jones's *Howl's Moving Castle*, Shirley Jackson's *We Have Always Lived in the Castle*
37. *Lethal White*: these are the 'Cormoran Strike' novels in order of publication
38. They are all buried in Highgate cemetery
39. *The Ghost Road*
40. Feathers: Max Porter, *Grief Is the Thing with Feathers*, Jacqueline Wilson, *Hetty Feather's Christmas* and A. E. W. Mason, *The Four Feathers*

---

* Larsson's diet reportedly consisted largely of cigarettes, processed food and copious amounts of coffee.
† I loved the *Peanuts* books as a child and was surprised and disappointed to find 'The Great Pumpkin' wasn't a real American Halloween tradition.
‡ Jeremy Dyson does not appear on screen in *The League of Gentlemen* but is co-creator with Mark Gatiss, Reece Shearsmith and Steve Pemberton.

41. *Pride and Prejudice* by Jane Austen
42. *Black Box Thinking* by Matthew Syed
43. *Cloud Atlas* by David Mitchell
44. *The Dice Man* by Luke Rhinehart
45. *The Mosquito Coast* by Paul Theroux
46. *The Miniaturist* (Miniature wrist) by Jessie Burton

# Quiz Number 11

**Round 1: This and That . . .** all the questions in this round are worth 1 point except question 10, which is worth 5.

1. **The First Question** – Which of these events is earliest in the calendar year in the UK: A) World Book Day, B) National Book Lovers Day or C) World Book Night?

2. **Anagram** – The anagram is always an author's name: HOUND CAN EAT LORRY

3. **Book Quote** – Can you name the book from which this quote comes? 'Nowadays people know the price of everything and the value of nothing.' Is it from: A) *Money* by Martin Amis, B) *The Picture of Dorian Gray* by Oscar Wilde, C) *Little Dorrit* by Charles Dickens or D) *What You See Is What You Get* by Alan Sugar?

4. Kingsmarkham is the fictional setting for which detective's series of books?

5. **Odd One Out** – Which of the following is not a real Sookie Stackhouse/*True Blood* series novel by Charlaine Harris: A) *From Dead to Worse*, B) *Dead and Gone*, C) *Definitely Dead* or D) *Dead and Breakfast*?

6. **Poetry Corner** – What is the next line? This quiz the poem is 'The Soldier' by Rupert Brooke: 'If I should die, think only this of me . . .'

7. **Fact or Fiction** – Which of the following is a fact about Maya Angelou. Is it: A) in her youth Maya was an actress and was close to getting the part of 'Uhura' in the original *Star Trek*, B) in her youth Maya Angelou

was a singer and released an LP in 1957 called *Miss Calypso* or C) in her youth Maya Angelou was an artist and one of her paintings now hangs in the White House?

8. This novel published in 1949 has led to two films (one starring John Hurt), two TV series, seven radio versions, several stage versions, an opera and a ballet, and was the subject of a never finished 1974 multimedia project for David Bowie. Can you name the book?

9. **What Year?** – In which year did these literary events take place? If you're playing in teams give a point to whichever team gets nearest. Born this year are: John Green, Chimamanda Ngozi Adichie and Jonathan Safran Foer. Nabokov and Terence Rattigan pass away this year. Published this year are Iris Murdoch's *The Sea, the Sea* and Toni Morrison's *Song of Solomon*. And Norman Mailer punches Gore Vidal in the face at a party in New York.

10. **Give Me Five** – Cressida Cowell is the eleventh Waterstones Children's Laureate (2019–21) but how many of the previous ten can you name? Five guesses, and a point for each that is correct.

**Round 2, Part A) Careful Now: Banned Books** – I'll give you the author's initials, the year of publication and the reason it was banned. A point for the title and a point for the author:

11. LC, 1865, banned in the province of Hunan, China (1931), for portraying animals acting on the same level as humans

12. SC, 1999, this book was banned in some American schools for being sexually explicit, anti-family, using offensive language, being unsuited to its age group, and including drugs, suicide and homosexuality

13. LFB, 1900, banned by many libraries in different American states for different reasons – in the South because of witches being referred to as 'good' and under McCarthyism for its perceived socialist values

14. ERB, 1912, banned from some US schools because the titular character was 'living in sin' with the character Jane

15. MS, 1963, banned from some US schools due to child psychologist Bruno Bettelheim stating (in *Ladies' Home Journal*) 'What the author failed to understand is the incredible fear it evokes in the child to be sent to bed without supper, and this by the first and foremost giver of food and security – his mother.'

**Round 2, Part B) Blankety Books** – Find the missing word: there's always a theme and this quiz the theme is . . . weather. A point for each one you get:

16. *The Shadow of the [Blank]* by Carlos Ruiz Zafón
17. *House of Sand and [Blank]* by Andre Dubus III
18. *Red [Blank] Rising* by Tom Clancy
19. *Summer [Blank]* by P. G. Wodehouse
20. *Gravity's [Blank]* by Thomas Pynchon

**Round 3, Part A) Two of a Kind** – I will describe a character and then an author. They share the same initials so if you know one it will help you get the other. A point for each you can name:

21. Character: From the 'Harry Potter' series who is murdered by Peter Pettigrew at the Little Hangleton graveyard; he was played in the films by Robert Pattinson. Author: The author of *On the Origin of Species*, published on 24 November 1859; he featured on the UK £10 note for eighteen years.

22. Character: The solicitor who travels to Transylvania to meet a foreign client by the name of Count Dracula who wishes to move to England, in Bram Stoker's 1897 novel. Author: The English author of *Chocolat*, *Five Quarters of the Orange* and the more recent *The Testament of Loki*.

23. Character: Beatrix Potter creation that features in the 1904 sequel to *The Tale of Peter Rabbit*; this character is Peter's cousin. Author: The English author born in Liverpool in 1932 who was nominated for the Booker Prize five times without winning, including for *The Dressmaker*, *An Awfully Big Adventure* and *The Bottle Factory Outing*; she was made a dame in 2000 and died in 2010.

24. Character: The human protagonist of Markus Zusak's 2005 hit *The Book Thief*; she's a young girl who steals books to protect them from the Nazis flames. Author: The Australian author of *Big Little Lies* and *Nine Perfect Strangers*; her older sister Jaclyn is also an author.

25. Character: And finally, the titular character of the novel by R. D. Blackmore, first published in 1869; the story's subtitle is *A Romance of Exmoor*. Author: The British novelist best known for the spy he created, Harry Palmer, who appears in *The Ipcress Files* and *Billion Dollar Brain*; he also wrote *SS-GB* and has written history and cookery books.

**Round 3, Part B) High Culture** – Questions about drugs in books, with a point for each correct answer:

26. Soma is a wonder drug from which Aldous Huxley novel of 1932?

27. In 2008, David Sheff's book about his son Nic's addiction to methamphetamine was published and was a

critical and commercial success. A film starring Steve Carell and Timothée Chalamet followed in 2018 – can you name the book?

28. Sci-fi classic *A Scanner Darkly* was published in 1977. The plot concerns Bob Arctor, an undercover police agent spying on his own household, who becomes addicted to 'Substance D' and must attempt rehab. The book was filmed in the 'rotoscope' style by Richard Linklater in 2006, but who wrote the original novel?

29. Which author, who often wrote of drug use, appears in the 1989 film *Drugstore Cowboy* and also recorded with Kurt Cobain?

30. Can you name Nelson Algren's classic 1949 novel about 'Frankie Machine', a gifted card dealer who becomes addicted to morphine. Frankie was played by Frank Sinatra in Otto Preminger's 1955 film version.

**Round 4, Part A) Connect 2** – Find the word that ends one title and starts the next. A point for each X you can identify and a point for each author:

31. *The Girl on the X Dreams*
32. *The Secret X Zigzag*
33. *The Shock of the X of Giants*
34. *Asterix and the Big X Club*
35. *Never Let Me X Tell It on the Mountain*

**Round 4, Part B) Literature Links and Lists** – Answer these novel conundrums for a point each:

36. What is the link between Philip Hensher's 2008 Booker-shortlisted novel based in Sheffield, Dave Eggers's 2013 dystopian novel, filmed in 2016 starring Tom Hanks, Elizabeth Smart's 1945 classic of prose poetry inspired

by her affair with George Baker and Guy Gunaratne's novel of 2019 that won the Dylan Thomas Prize?

37. What appears in the title of books by Doris Lessing, Walt Whitman and John Christopher?

38. What connects the authors of *M Train*, *Naked at the Albert Hall* and *Reckless*?

39. Complete this trilogy: *City of Glass*, *Ghosts* and . . .?

40. Gary Oldman, Denholm Elliot and Alec Guinness have all played the same character on film – who created that character?

Finally, there are six 'SayWhatYouSee' visual representations of novels. Give yourself a point for the author and a point for the title.

Total up your answers and see how many you got.

The highest score possible on this quiz is 76

Thanks for playing!

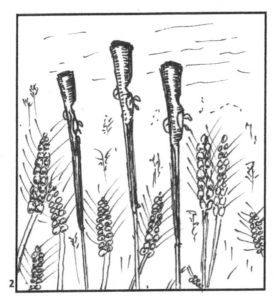

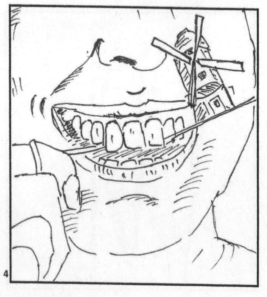

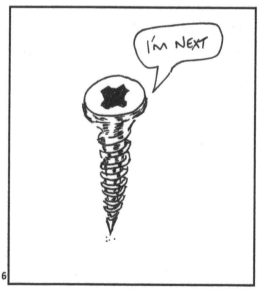

# The Answers

1. A) World Book Day, 5 March (World Book Night, 23 April, National Book Lovers Day, 9 August)
2. Arthur Conan Doyle
3. B) *The Picture of Dorian Gray* by Oscar Wilde
4. Inspector Wexford by Ruth Rendell
5. *Dead and Breakfast* (that is a Kate Kingsbury novel)
6. 'That there's some corner of a foreign field
   That is for ever England.'
7. B) She released an LP called *Miss Calypso**
8. *1984* by George Orwell[†]
9. 1977
10. Quentin Blake was the first Children's Laureate (1999–2001), followed by Anne Fine (2001–3), Michael Morpurgo (2003–5), Jacqueline Wilson (2005–7), Michael Rosen (2007–9), Anthony Browne (2009–11), Julia Donaldson (2011–13), Malorie Blackman (2013–15), Chris Riddell (2015–17) and Lauren Child (2017–19)[‡]

* She was the first black female conductor on San Francisco's streetcars; and she was also an actress, director and producer of plays, movies and television shows.
† Orwell's widow refused Bowie the rights to use it; many of the songs from the project appeared on Bowie's *Diamond Dogs* LP.
‡ The idea for a Children's Laureate came from (then Poet Laureate) Ted Hughes and Michael Morpurgo. The Children's Laureate receives a bursary of £15,000 and a specially designed and inscribed silver medal.

11. *Alice's Adventures in Wonderland* by Lewis Carroll
12. *The Perks of Being a Wallflower* by Stephen Chbosky
13. *The Wonderful Wizard of Oz* by L. Frank Baum
14. *Tarzan of the Apes* by Edgar Rice Burroughs
15. *Where the Wild Things Are* by Maurice Sendak*
16. *Wind*
17. *Fog*
18. *Storm*
19. *Lightning*
20. *Rainbow*
21. Cedric Diggory and Charles Darwin
22. Jonathan Harker and Joanne Harris
23. Benjamin Bunny and Beryl Bainbridge
24. Liesel Meminger and Liane Moriarty
25. Lorna Doone and Len Deighton
26. *Brave New World*
27. *Beautiful Boy: A Father's Journey Through His Son's Addiction* (the film also contained elements from Nic's book, *Tweak: Growing Up on Methamphetamines*)
28. Philip K. Dick
29. William S. Burroughs
30. *The Man with the Golden Arm*
31. *Train*, Paula Hawkins and Denis Johnson
32. *Agent*, Joseph Conrad and Ben Macintyre
33. *Fall*, Nathan Filer and Ken Follett
34. *Fight*, Goscinny & Uderzo and Chuck Palahniuk
35. *Go*, Kazuo Ishiguro and James Baldwin
36. London tube lines: *The **Northern** Clemency* by Philip Hensher, *The **Circle*** by Dave Eggers, *By Grand **Central***

---

* I didn't include it here but *Harriet the Spy* by Louise Fitzhugh (1964) was also banned from some libraries for various reasons: that it taught children to lie, back talk and curse, but also that it taught them to 'spy' – I suppose that point couldn't really be argued.

*Station I Sat Down and Wept* by Elizabeth Smart and *In Our Mad and Furious **City*** by Guy Gunaratne

37. Grass: *The Grass is Singing* by Doris Lessing; *Leaves of Grass* by Walt Whitman and *The Death of Grass* by John Christopher

38. All female singers: Patti Smith, Tracey Thorn and Chrissie Hynde

39. *The Locked Room*, all originally published as Paul Auster's *New York Trilogy*

40. John le Carré; the character is George Smiley

41. *Grapes of Wrath* by John Steinbeck

42. *The Three Musketeers* (Musket ears of corn) by Alexandre Dumas

43. *Decline and Fall* by Evelyn Waugh

44. *The Mill on the Floss* by George Eliot

45. *Interview with the Vampire* by Anne Rice

46. *The Turn of the Screw* by Henry James

# Quiz Number 12

**Round 1: This and that . . .** all the questions in this round are worth 1 point except question 10, which is worth 5.

1. **The First Question** – Which of these books was published first: A) Jon Klassen's *I Want My Hat Back*, B) Dr Seuss's *The Cat in the Hat* or C) Sue Kendra's *Keith the Cat with the Magic Hat*?

2. **Anagram** – The anagram is always an author's name: UNPAID RUM HEADER

3. **Book Quote** – Can you name the book from which this quote comes? 'You are here for but an instant, and you mustn't take yourself too seriously.' Is it from: A) *The Time Machine* by H. G. Wells, B) *Peter Pan* by J. M. Barrie, C) *The Land That Time Forgot* by Edgar Rice Burroughs or D) *Will* by Will Self?

4. At which university was Philip Larkin a librarian from 1955 until his death in 1985?

5. **Odd One Out** – Which of the following is not a real Bernard Cornwell novel: A) *Sharpe's Fury*, B) *Sharpe Objects*, C) *Sharpe's Revenge* or D) *Sharpe's Havoc*?

6. **Poetry Corner** – What is the next line? This quiz the poem is 'Auguries of Innocence' by William Blake: 'To see a World in a Grain of Sand . . .'

7. **Fact or Fiction** – Which of the following is a fact about Ali Smith: A) Ali Smith was part of the St Winifred's School Choir who had a hit in 1980 with 'There's No One Quite Like Grandma', B) Ali Smith was once a part-time

lettuce cleaner or C) Ali Smith once turned down a Baileys Women's Prize nomination as she is strictly teetotal?

8. This sci-fi classic was published in 1898 and was famously adapted for radio in 1938; it was first made into a film in 1953, an album in 1978, then another film in 2005 and a stage musical in 2006. The latest adaptation was a BBC TV series in 2019 starring Rafe Spall. Can you name the book?

9. **What Year?** – In which year did these literary events take place? If you're playing in teams give a point to whichever team gets nearest. A good year for Tolkien fans as his translation of *Beowulf* has its first publication and the third and final Hobbit film by Peter Jackson is released at the cinema. Also published this year are Jessie Burton's *The Miniaturist* and Kate Atkinson's *A God in Ruins*. *The Narrow Road to the Deep North* by Richard Flanagan wins the Man Booker Prize, and Sue Townsend and P. D. James both pass away.

10. **Give Me Five** – How many of the Wombles can you name? Name five of the main characters from Elisabeth Beresford's five novels and one short-story collection and get yourself 5 points!

## Round 2, Part A) Music in Books and Books in Music
– A point for each correct answer:

11. Which rock legend released his autobiography called *Thanks a lot Mr Kibblewhite* in 2018?

12. What book was Mark Chapman holding when he shot John Lennon?

13. What is the name of the record shop in Nick Hornby's *High Fidelity*?

14. The band the Airborne Toxic Event take their name from which Don DeLillo novel?

15. Which Smiths song did Douglas Coupland name a book after?

**Round 2, Part B) Blankety Books** – Find the missing word: there's always a theme and this quiz the theme is ... Cluedo! A point for each one you get:

16. *Anne of [Blank] Gables* by L. M. Montgomery
17. *[Blank] Pie* by P. G. Wodehouse
18. *The Ivory [Blank]* by Patricia Wentworth
19. *The [Blank] Emporium* by Jojo Moyes
20. *The Swimming-Pool [Blank]* by Alan Hollinghurst

**Round 3, Part A) Two of a Kind** – I will describe a character and then an author, They share the same initials so if you know one it will help you get the other. A point for each you can name:

21. Character: This character appears in *Ulysses* by James Joyce; she is an opera singer; she is the wife of Leopold and the mother of Milly and Rudy, and is having an affair with Hugh 'Blazes' Boylan. Author: The author of the popular and highly acclaimed 'Noughts and Crosses' series – which was adapted for the BBC in 2020; she was the Children's Laureate from 2013 to 2015 and was made an OBE in 2008.
22. Character: The character created in 1930 by Edward Stratemeyer as a female counterpart to his popular 'Hardy Boys' series of detective stories; she has been brought to the screen a number of times, including a very popular TV series on ABC in the US in the late 1970s starring Pamela Sue Martin; for her ninetieth anniversary her 'death' is investigated by the Hardy Boys. Author: The author and playwright born in London best known

for her era-defining 1967 novel *Poor Cow* and her short-story collection *Up the Junction* from 1963; she also wrote the play *Steaming* (1981) that won the best new comedy at the Society of West End Theatre Awards (now known as the Laurence Olivier Awards).

23. Character: The main protagonist and narrator of Veronica Roth's 'Divergent' series, she was played in the film adaptation by Shailene Woodley. Author: The late author of the hugely popular 'Discworld' series. He also collaborated with Stephen Baxter on the 'Long Earth' series and Neil Gaiman on *Good Omens*.

24. Character: Initially Frodo's gardener he becomes his strongest ally in Tolkien's *The Lord of the Rings*. Author: The American author of the bestselling 'Alphabet' series of crime books, *A is for Alibi*, *B is for Burglar* and so on, who died in 2017.

25. Character: And finally, Rick Riordan's creation who is the son of a mortal woman and the god Poseidon; he first appears aged twelve in 2005's *The Lightning Thief*. Author: The bestselling crime writer of the 'Roy Grace' novels, which have sold over 19 million copies world-wide and given him twelve consecutive *Sunday Times* no. 1s.

**Round 3, Part B) Well Red** – All these books have a shade of red in the title. I'll give you the author, the year of publication and the initials of the title, Just tell me the title for a point:

26. Nathaniel Hawthorne, TSL, 1850
27. Michel Faber, TCPATW, 2002
28. Jeanette Winterson, STC, 1989
29. Philipp Meyer, AR, 2009
30. Philip Pullman, TRITS, 1985

**Round 4, Part A) If I Do Say So Myself** – British celebrity autobiographies, I will give you the title and the year just name the celebrity for a point:

31. *Nerd Do Well*, 2009
32. *At My Mother's Knee . . . and Other Low Joints*, 2008
33. *Who Am I Again?*, 2019
34. *Me*, 2019
35. *My Word Is My Bond*, 2008

**Round 4, Part B) Literature Links and Lists** – Answer these novel conundrums for a point each:

36. In which country were George Orwell, William Thackery and Rudyard Kipling all born?
37. What comes next in this list: *Out of Oz, A Lion Among Men, Son of a Witch* . . .?
38. What is the specific link between *My Wicked, Wicked Ways* by Errol Flynn, *A Moveable Feast* by Ernest Hemingway and *My Life with Earth Wind and Fire* by Maurice White?
39. What is the link between Arthur Conan Doyle, Michael Crichton, Anton Chekhov and Harry Hill?
40. Which famous TV science-fiction character connects Jenny T, Colgan, Michael Moorcock and A. L. Kennedy?

Finally, there are six 'SayWhatYouSee' visual representations of novels. Give yourself a point for the author and a point for the title.

Then total up your answers and see how many you scored.
    The highest score possible on this quiz is 61.
    Thanks for playing!

# The Answers

1. B) *The Cat in the Hat*, 1957 (*I Want My Hat Back*, 2011, *Keith the Cat with the Magic Hat*, 2012)
2. Daphne du Maurier
3. C) *The Land that Time Forgot* by Edgar Rice Burroughs
4. Hull
5. B) *Sharpe Objects* (*Sharp Objects* is by Gillian Flynn)
6. 'And a Heaven in a Wild Flower'
7. B) She was a part-time lettuce cleaner in her youth
8. *The War of the Worlds* by H. G. Wells
9. 2014
10. The main seven are: Great Uncle Bulgaria (full name Bulgaria Coburg Womble), Tobermory, Madame Cholet, Orinoco, Wellington, Tomsk and Bungo*
11. Roger Daltrey
12. *The Catcher in the Rye* by J. D. Salinger

* But there are many more – Alderney, Shansi, Stepney, Cairngorm MacWomble the Terrible, Obidos, Miss Adelaide, Nanny Alexandria, Cousin Van Amsterdam, Ms Atlanta, Bermondsey, Onkel Bonn, Cousin Botany, Cairns, Culvain, Uncle Dunedin, Eucula, Chieftain Fashven, Frau Heidelberg, Heilbronn, Workshop Master Hirado, Hoboken, Great-Great-Great Uncle Hohenzollern (Hapsburg Von Hohenzollern Womble), Idaho, Tante Lille, Livingstone, Moosonee, Great-Great Aunt Matilda Murrumbidgee, Nanking, Omsk, Cousin Ontario, Perth, Quetta, Serengeti, Speyer, Stromboli, Great Aunt Thessaly, Honourable Cousin Tokyo, Winnipeg, Woy Woy, Cousin Yellowstone (full name Yellowstone Boston Womble)!

13. Championship Vinyl
14. *White Noise*
15. 'Girlfriend in a Coma'
16. *Green*: Reverend Green, suspect
17. *Plum*: Professor Plum, suspect
18. *Dagger*: possible weapon
19. *Peacock*: Mrs Peacock, suspect
20. *Library*: possible location
21. Molly Bloom and Malorie Blackman
22. Nancy Drew and Nell Dunn
23. Tris Prior and Terry Pratchett
24. Samwise Gamgee and Sue Grafton*
25. Percy Jackson and Peter James
26. *The Scarlet Letter*
27. *The Crimson Petal and the White*
28. *Sexing the Cherry*
29. *American Rust*
30. *The Ruby in the Smoke*
31. Simon Pegg
32. Paul O'Grady
33. Lenny Henry
34. Elton John
35. Roger Moore†
36. India
37. *Wicked: The Life and Times of the Wicked Witch of the West* by Gregory Maguire: these are 'The Wicked Years' in reverse publication order

---

* Sue Grafton had reached *Y is for Yesterday* but sadly passed away before she could complete the Z title (in case you're wondering, the X book is simply called *X*).
† I couldn't include this as the title is a giveaway, but you have to love the title of Shane Richie's autobiography from 2003: *Rags to Richie*.

38. They are all posthumously released autobiographies
39. All qualified as medical doctors
40. Doctor Who – they have all written standalone *Doctor Who*-related books
41. *Rooster Bar* by John Grisham
42. *Wise Children* (Y's Children) by Angela Carter
43. *The Crying of Lot 49* by Thomas Pynchon
44. *Red Dragon* by Thomas Harris
45. *House of Leaves* by Mark Z. Danielewski
46. *The Tipping Point* by Malcom Gladwell

# Quiz Number 13

**Round 1: This and that . . .** all the questions in this round are worth 1 point except question 10, which is worth 5.

1. **The First Question** – Which of these authors called Alice was born first: A) Alice Munro, B) Alice Sebold or C) Alice Walker?

2. **Anagram** – The anagram is always an author's name: SCROLL WAILER

3. **Book Quote** – Can you name the book from which this quote comes? 'Life is like a shit sandwich. The more bread you've got, the less shit you have to eat.' Is it from: A) *The Debt* by Roberta Kray, B) *Dangerous Lady* by Martina Cole, C) *Layer Cake* by J. J. Connolly or D) *The Weekend Baker* by Paul Hollywood?

4. True or false: Thomas Pynchon's middle name is Biggles.

5. **Odd One Out** – Which of the following is not a real Robert Ludlum thriller: A) *The Scorpio Illusion*, B) *The Icarus Agenda*, C) *The Fionavar Tapestry* or D) *The Prometheus Deception*?

6. **Poetry Corner** – What is the next line? This quiz the poem is 'Casabianca' by Felicia Hemans: 'The boy stood on the burning deck . . .'

7. **Fact or Fiction** – Which of the following is a fact about John Irving: A) John Irving's first job was as a circus clown; he ran away from home to join the circus and lasted two weeks, B) John Irving took up wrestling as a

student and wrestled in tournaments until he was thirty-four or C) John Irving is a talented guitar player and in 1965 he auditioned for the Monkees?

8. Is Boy George's autobiography from 1995 called: A) *Do You Really Want to Know Me?*, B) *Take It Like a Man* or C) *Taboo*?

9. **What Year?** – In which year did these literary events take place? If you're playing in teams give a point to whichever team gets nearest. Born this year: Joanne Harris and Carlos Ruiz Zafón. Ian Fleming dies. The first 'Flat Stanley' book by Jeff Brown is published, as is *Herzog* by Saul Bellow and *Last Exit to Brooklyn* by Hubert Selby Jr. Jean-Paul Sartre was awarded the Nobel Prize in Literature and promptly refused it. He said he always refused official distinctions and did not want to be 'institutionalised'.

10. **Give Me Five** – This quiz it's the Moomins. Tove Jansson created nine books and five picture books (and a comic strip) – can you name five of the main characters for 5 points?

**Round 2, Part A) Clickbait Books** – Book plots reimagined as 'clickbait' headlines. Name the book for a point and take a point for the author:

11. 'This crazy hermit lures children into his factory and punishes them for minor faults!'

12. 'How a normal business trip to Transylvania turned into a nightmare this man will never forget!'

13. 'Drop a bunch of good kids on a desert island – how bad could it get? Find out here!'

14. 'This genius spider saved this pig's life but at what cost?'

15. 'This greedy insect couldn't stop eating, you won't believe what happens next!'

**Round 2, Part B) Blankety Books** – Find the missing word: there's always a theme and this quiz the theme is ... London tube stations. A point for each one you get:

16. *Miss Garnet's [Blank]* by Sally Vickers
17. *The Piano Shop on the Left [Blank]* by T. E. Carhart
18. *[Blank] to Murder* by Mari Hannah
19. *The [Blank] of the Golden Pavilion* by Yukio Mishima
20. *How the French Won [Blank] or Think They Did* by Tim Clarke

**Round 3, Part A) Two of a Kind** – I will describe a character and then an author. They share the same initials so if you know one it will help you get the other. A point for each you can name.

21. Character: The male protagonist of one of Shakespeare's greatest tragedies; his love for Juliet causes familial issues. Author: The author of classic sci-fi such as *The Shrinking Man* and *I Am Legend*; he also adapted his own short story, 'Duel', for Spielberg's first feature film.
22. Character: The titular character from Charles Dickens's 1850 novel that also features Betsey Trotwood and Uriah Heep; Armando Iannucci adapted the book for film in 2019, with Dev Patel taking the lead. Author: The German-born Canadian author probably best known for *Generation X* and *Girlfriend in a Coma*.
23. Character: The main protagonist of Ernest Hemingway's *For Whom the Bell Tolls*, this book, published in 1940, tells the story of an American volunteer in the Spanish Civil War and it was published just after the end of that conflict. Author: The penname of the fantasy author best known for his 'The Wheel of Time' series; he also wrote 'Conan the Barbarian' novels (and much more).

24. Character: The character created by Robert Ludlum whose real name is David Webb; in his first appearance he has amnesia and in the film version of that book he is played by Matt Damon. Author: The American author considered to be one of the earliest writers to tackle teenage issues and who is best known for *Are You There God? It's Me, Margaret.*

25. Character: And finally, the aloof romantic interest of Elizabeth Bennet in *Pride and Prejudice* by Jane Austen. Author: The nineteenth-century Russian author of *Crime and Punishment* and *The Brothers Karamazov.*

**Round 3, Part B) It's a Date!** – I'll give you the fictional event and the author. Just tell me the title for a point:

26. 5 February 1933: Franklin Roosevelt is assassinated by Giuseppe Zangara in this novel by Philip K. Dick from 1962

27. 1 January 1975: Archie Jones decides not to kill himself in this novel by Zadie Smith from 2000.

28. 24 April (year not stated): Bunny Corcoran disappears in this novel by Donna Tartt from 1992.

29. 8 January 1960: Calliope Stephanides is born 19 inches long, weighing 7 pounds and 4 ounces, and is assigned female in this novel by Jeffrey Eugenides from 2002.

30. 29 June 1931: The date of Frobisher's first letter to Sixsmith in this novel by David Mitchell from 2004.

**Round 4, Part A) Characters** – I will list some key characters from a book. Just name the book for a point and the author for another:

31. Ben Gunn, Billy Bones and Captain Smollett

32. Dennis, Raj, Lisa and Mr Hawtrey

33. Jo, Amy, Beth and Meg
34. Raoul Duke and Dr Gonzo
35. Cora, Francis, William and Luke

**Round 4, Part B) Literature Links and Lists** – Answer these novel conundrums for a point each:

36. Which American state links *All the Pretty Horses* by Cormac McCarthy, *The Son* by Philipp Meyer and *Friday Night Lights* by H. G. Bissinger?
37. What links these books: *The Vegetarian* by Han Kang, *A Horse Walks into a Bar* by David Grossman and *Flights* by Olga Tokarczuk?
38. What links books by Ellis Peters, James Runcie and G. K. Chesterton?
39. What comes next in this trilogy: *Identity, Supremacy . . .*?
40. What links a telekinetic prom queen, a St Bernard that has been bitten by a rabid bat and Paul Sheldon, a kidnapped author?

Finally, there are six 'SayWhatYouSee' visual representations of novels. Give yourself a point for the author and a point for the title.

Total up your answers and see how many you scored.

The highest score possible on this quiz is 66.

Thanks for playing!

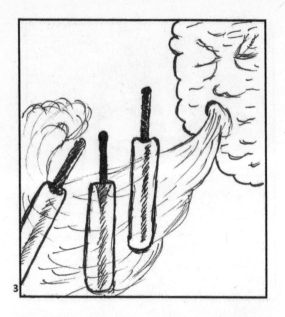

# The Answers

1. A) Alice Munro, 1931 (Alice Walker, 1944, Alice Sebold, 1962)
2. Lewis Carroll
3. B) Martina Cole's *Dangerous Lady*
4. False, it's Ruggles
5. C) *The Fionavar Tapestry* (this is a book by Guy Gavriel Kay)
6. 'Whence all but he had fled'
7. B) Irving was a wrestler*
8. B) *Take It Like a Man*
9. 1964[†]
10. Moomintroll, also referred to as 'Moomin' in some of the English translations, Moominpappa, Moominmamma, Little My, Sniff, Snork Maiden, Snufkin, the younger Mymble, also referred to as 'the Mymble's daughter', Snork (Snork Maiden's brother), Too-Ticky, Stinky
11. *Charlie and the Chocolate Factory* by Roald Dahl

* 'Wrestling requires extreme dedication, self-punishing behavior and devout concentration on the repetition of small details,' Irving said. 'You learn something unnatural until it is natural. Writing a novel that may take you five or six or seven years is a lot like being wrestler.' (From Intermatwrestle.com's profile of John Irving)

† Fleming's last recorded words are an apology to the ambulance drivers for having inconvenienced them. He said – 'I am sorry to trouble you chaps. I don't know how you get along so fast with the traffic on the roads these days.'

12. *Dracula* by Bram Stoker
13. *Lord of the Flies* by William Golding
14. *Charlotte's Web* by E. B. White
15. *The Very Hungry Caterpillar* by Eric Carle
16. *Angel*
17. *Bank*
18. *Monument*
19. *Temple*
20. *Waterloo*
21. Romeo Montague and Richard Matheson
22. David Copperfield and Douglas Coupland
23. Well it's Robert Jordan and ... Robert Jordan! They share the same name
24. Jason Bourne and Judy Blume
25. Fitzwilliam Darcy and Fyodor Dostoevsky
26. *The Man in the High Castle*
27. *White Teeth*
28. *The Secret History*
29. *Middlesex*
30. *Cloud Atlas*
31. *Treasure Island* by R. L. Stevenson
32. *The Boy in the Dress* by David Walliams
33. *Little Women* by Louisa May Alcott
34. *Fear and Loathing in Las Vegas* by Hunter S. Thompson
35. *The Essex Serpent* by Sarah Perry
36. Texas
37. They have all won the International Man Booker Prize
38. They all created crime-combatting clergy: Ellis Peters created Cadfael, James Runcie wrote the 'Grantchester' books and G. K. Chesterton created Father Brown
39. *Ultimatum*: these are Robert Ludlum's Bourne books in publication order
40. Stephen King: these are all subjects of his books (*Carrie*, *Cujo* and *Misery*)

41. *Brideshead Revisited* by Evelyn Waugh
42. *Cold Comfort Farm* by Stella Gibbons
43. *The Wind in the Willows* by Kenneth Grahame
44. *The Horse Whisperer* by Nicholas Evans
45. *The Last of the Mohicans* by James Fennimore Cooper
46. *The Secrets of Chimneys* by Agatha Christie

# Quiz Number 14

**Round 1: This and That . . .** all the questions in this round are worth 1 point except question 10, which is worth 5.

1. **The First Question** – Which of these fictional bears was the first to feature in a full-length cinema released film: A) Paddington Bear, B) Winnie the Pooh or C) Baloo from *The Jungle Book*?

2. **Anagram** – The anagram is always an author's name: A BITTER EXPORT

3. **Book Quote** – Can you name the book from which this quote comes? 'We call them dumb animals, and so they are, for they cannot tell us how they feel, but they do not suffer less because they have no words.' Is it from: A) *Black Beauty* by Anna Sewell, B) *Charlotte's Web* by E. B. White, C) *Under the Skin* by Michel Faber or D) *Have I Got Views for You* by Boris Johnson?

4. Who said, 'You can never get a cup of tea large enough or a book long enough to suit me': A) Alan Bennett, B) Lewis Carroll or C) C. S. Lewis?

5. **Odd One Out** – Which of the following is not a real Enid Blyton book: A) *Five on a Treasure Island*, B) *Five Meet Mr Pink-Whistle*, C) *Five Have Plenty of Fun* or D) *Five Go to Billycock Hill*?

6. **Poetry Corner** – What is the next line? This quiz the poem is 'The Arrow and the Song' by Henry Wadsworth Longfellow: 'I shot an arrow into the air . . .'

7. **Fact or Fiction** – Which of the following is a fact about Hans Christian Andersen: A) Andersen was a very nervous traveller, so he always travelled with a coil of rope in case he needed to escape out of a window, B) despite 'The Ugly Duckling' being one of his best-known works, Andersen suffered from severe ornithophobia and would in fact run away if approached by a duck or C) Andersen was fascinated with Joseph Merrick aka 'the Elephant man' and he asked his friend Dickens to arrange a meeting – but Dickens declined?

8. This 1959 novel was most famously adapted into a film in 1963, directed by John Schlesinger and starring Tom Courtenay in the title role. Courtenay had been understudy to Albert Finney in the stage version that opened in London's West End in 1960. The book was also turned into a TV series that ran from 1973 to 1974. There was also a musical and a sequel to the book was published in 1975, where the character was 'on the Moon'. Can you name the book?

9. **What Year?** – In which year did these literary events take place? If you're playing in teams give a point to whichever team gets nearest. Margaret Atwood wins the Man Booker for *The Blind Assassin*. Philip Pullman's *The Amber Spyglass* and Michael Chabon's *The Amazing Adventures of Kavalier and Clay* are published. Illustrator Edward Gorey and *Peanuts* creator Charles M. Schulz both pass away and Jeffrey Archer is charged with perjury.

10. **Give Me Five** – Name as many of the late great Iain Banks's fourteen novels as you can (not including his science-fiction novels published under the name Iain M. Banks). Five correct answers gets you 5 points!

**Round 2, Part A) Awesome Alliterative Authors** – I will give you their date of birth, the title of their first published work and the initial with which their names begin. Just name the author for a point:

11. Born 8 November 1900, first book was *Gone with the Wind*, and the letter is M.
12. Born 2 January 1951, first book was *Call Me By Your Name*, and the letter is A.
13. Born 19 March 1978, first book was called *What Belongs to You*, and the letter is G
14. Born 24 July 1978, first book was *The Song of Achilles*, and the letter is M.
15. Born 20 November 1936, first book was *Americana*, and the letter is D.

**Round 2, Part B) Blankety Books** – Find the missing word: there's always a theme and this quiz the theme is . . . shapes. A point for each one you get:

16. *The Closed [Blank]* by Jonathan Coe
17. *The [Blank] Hunters* by Wilbur Smith
18. *Hangover [Blank]* by Patrick Hamilton
19. *The [Blank] is a Lonely Hunter* by Carson McCullers
20. *The Fault in Our [Blanks]* by John Green

**Round 3, Part A) Two of a Kind** – I will describe a character and then an author. They share the same initials so if you know one it will help you get the other. A point for each you can name:

21. Character: The famous magical nanny created by P. T. Travers in 1934; Travers wrote seven sequels, the final one in 1988 when she was eighty-nine. Author: The

American author and journalist best known for his 1969 novel *The Godfather*.

22. Character: Edward St Aubyn's semi-autobiographical character who has appeared in five novels and was portrayed in a Sky TV series by Benedict Cumberbatch. Author: This author's works include *Something for the Weekend* and two 'Jenny Q' books but she is better known as an actress and most famously as Mrs Doyle from the series *Father Ted*.

23. Character: The police officer/bounty hunter who hunts replicants in Philip K. Dick's *Do Androids Dream of Electric Sheep?*; he was played by Harrison Ford in the film version *Blade Runner*. Author: The British author, ethologist and evolutionary biologist best known for books such as *The Selfish Gene* and *The God Delusion*.

24. Character: The character who is whisked from Kansas to Oz with her dog Toto in L. Frank Baum's *The Wonderful Wizard of Oz* in 1900; I think everyone knows her first name, but do you know the surname too? Author: The American author best known for his 1994 novel *Snow Falling on Cedars*, which was filmed in 1999 starring Ethan Hawke.

25. Character: A Professor at Hogwarts, in the first 'Harry Potter' book he is the school's potion master and he was portrayed in all the film versions by Alan Rickman. Author: The American author of eighteen novels, such as *If Tomorrow Comes* and *Windmills of the Gods*, that sold over 300 million copies; he was also a TV producer and created *I Dream of Jeannie* and *Hart to Hart*.

**Round 3, Part B) What the Dickens!** – Are these real Dickens characters or what? Say (or write) Dickens! if it's real and What! if I made it up. A point for each time you are correct:

26. Decimus Tite Barnacle
27. Hiram Grewgious
28. Helena de Chair
29. Frederick Frightwig
30. Uncle Pumblechook

**Round 4, Part A) Cup of Books** – If two books 'played' each other, which would win (i.e. which book has the higher number in the title)? I will give you the authors and titles – minus the numbers of course. Just name the winner! (Bonus points if you know the numbers)

31. Charles Dickens's *A Tale of X Cities* v. Liane Moriarty's *X Wishes*
32. Kate Atkinson's *X Good Turn'* v. Agatha Christie's *The X Dials Mystery*
33. Patricia Highsmith's *The X Faces of January* v. Mitch Albom's *The X People You Meet in Heaven*
34. Pittacus Lore's *I Am Number X* v. Michael Connelly's *X Kinds of Truth*
35. Stephen King's *From a Buick X* v. Claire North's *The First X Lives of Harry August*

**Round 4, Part B) Literature Links and Lists** – Answer these novel conundrums for a point each:

36. In which country were these authors born: Thomas Mann, W. G. Sebald, Bernhard Schlink and Patrick Süskind?
37. What is next in this list: *The Long Cosmos*, *The Long Utopia*, *The Long Mars*, *The Long War* . . .?

38. What specifically links Gertrude Stein, Collette, Marcel Proust and Oscar Wilde?
39. What links the surname of Rebecca from Daphne du Maurier's novel, Rachel Carson's book on the dangers of pesticides from 1962, Shakespeare's play featuring Puck and Bottom and David Mitchell's novel concerning Jacob de Zoet?
40. Which meal features in titles by Truman Capote, Kurt Vonnegut and Jacqueline Wilson?

Finally, there are six 'SayWhatYouSee' visual representations of novels. Give yourself a point for the author and a point for the title.

Total up your answers and see how many you scored.
   The highest score possible on this quiz is 71.
   Thanks for playing!

# The Answers

1. C) Baloo, 1967 (Winnie the Pooh, 1977, Paddington, 2014)*
2. Beatrix Potter
3. A) *Black Beauty* by Anna Sewell
4. C) C. S. Lewis†
5. B) *Five Meet Mr Pink-Whistle* ('Mr Pink-Whistle' was another Blyton creation but there was no crossover)
6. 'It fell to earth, I knew not where'
7. A) He was nervous traveller‡
8. *Billy Liar* by Keith Waterhouse
9. 2000
10. *The Wasp Factory, Walking on Glass, The Bridge, Espedair Street, Canal Dreams, The Crow Road, Complicity, Whit, A Song of Stone, The Business, Dead Air, The Steep Approach to Garbadale, Stonemouth, The Quarry*
11. Margaret Mitchell
12. André Aciman
13. Garth Greenwell

* Winnie the Pooh was in a short featurette called *Winnie the Pooh and the Honey Tree* in 1966 but his first feature film wasn't until 1977 – *The Many Adventures of Winnie the Pooh*.
† I would have put money on this being Alan Bennett, but I would have lost it.
‡ He was friends with Dickens, up to a point – the point where Dickens thought he had outstayed his welcome. Andersen asked to visit Dickens for two weeks, which turned into five. Dickens was not impressed.

14. Madeline Miller
15. Don DeLillo
16. *Circle*
17. *Diamond*
18. *Square*
19. *Heart*
20. *Stars*
21. Mary Poppins and Mario Puzo
22. Patrick Melrose and Pauline McLynn
23. Rick Deckard and Richard Dawkins
24. Dorothy Gale and David Guterson
25. Severus Snape and Sidney Sheldon
26. Dickens! (from *Little Dorrit*)
27. Dickens! (from *The Mystery of Edwin Drood*)*
28. What! (this is actually Jacob Rees-Mogg's wife)
29. What!
30. Dickens! (from *Great Expectations*)
31. Lianne Moriarty wins 2–3 (*A Tale of Two Cities* and *Three Wishes*)
32. Agatha Christie wins easily 1–7 (*One Good Turn* and *The Seven Dials Mystery*)
33. An away win for Mitch Albom 2–5 (*The Two Faces of January* and *The Five People You Meet in Heaven*)
34. A win for Pittacus Lore 4–2 (*I Am Number Four* and *Two Kinds of Truth*)
35. Claire North is the champ 8–15, what a game! (*From a Buick 8* and *The First Fifteen Lives of Harry August*)
36. Germany
37. *The Long Earth*: Terry Pratchett and Stephen Baxter's 'Long Earth' series in reverse publication order
38. All buried in Père-Lachaise Cemetery in Paris

* This name is an anagram of 'Gregarious Whim'.

39. Seasons: Rebecca de **Winter**, *Silent* **Spring**, *A Mid**summer** Night's Dream* and *The Thousand **Autumns*** *of Jacob de Zoet*)

40. Breakfast: Truman Capote's *Breakfast at Tiffany's*, Kurt Vonnegut's *Breakfast of Champions* and Jacqueline Wilson's *The Bed and Breakfast Star*

41. *The Postman Always Rings Twice* by James M. Cain

42. *Stardust* by Neil Gaiman

43. *No Country for Old Men* by Cormac McCarthy

44. *Call for the Dead* by John Le Carre

45. *The Book of Laughter and Forgetting* by Milan Kundera

46. *The Maltese Falcon* by Dashiell Hammett

# Quiz Number 15

**Round 1: This and that . . .** all the questions in this round are worth 1 point except question 10, which is worth 5.

1. **The First Question** – Which of these was published first: A) *Born to Run* by Michael Morpurgo, B) *What I Talk About When I Talk About Running* by Haruki Murakami or C) *The Loneliness of the Long-distance Runner* by Alan Sillitoe?

2. **Anagram** – The anagram is always an author's name: I AM A FULL WRINKLE

3. **Book Quote** – Can you name the book from which this quote comes? 'I felt that Tom would drift on forever seeking a little wistfully for the dramatic turbulence of some irrecoverable football game.' Is it from: A) *The History of Tom Jones* by Henry Fielding, B) *The Great Gatsby* by F. Scott Fitzgerald, C) *The Talented Mr Ripley* by Patricia Highsmith or D) *Both Feet on the Ground* by David Beckham?

4. Which comedian released the novel *Mr Lonely* in 1981 – his only novel to be published in his lifetime?

5. **Odd One Out** – Which of the following is not a real James Herbert novel: A) *The Fog*, B) *The Dark*, C) *Slugs* or D) *The Rats*?

6. **Poetry Corner** – What is the next line? This quiz the poem is 'Do Not Go Gentle into that Good Night' by Dylan Thomas: 'Do not go gentle into that good night . . .'

7. **Fact or Fiction** –Which of the following is a fact about Kurt Vonnegut: A) Kurt Vonnegut opened the first Saab dealership in the US, B) Kurt Vonnegut opened the first record shop in New York after being unable to find his beloved jazz records or C) Kurt Vonnegut bankrolled the very first Barnes & Noble store in Minnesota?

8. Which author's last words were reportedly, 'Does Nobody understand?'

9. **What Year?** – In which year did these literary events take place? If you're playing in teams give a point to whichever team gets nearest. Published this year: Hunter S. Thompson's *Fear and Loathing in Las Vegas*, Roald Dahl's *Charlie and the Great Glass Elevator* and Tove Jansson's *The Summer Book*. China Miéville is born, Ezra Pound and Cecil Day-Lewis pass away and Sir John Betjeman is appointed Poet Laureate. The highest grossing film of the year is Francis Ford Coppola's film of Mario Puzo's *The Godfather*.

10. **Give Me Five** – Many consider Graham Greene to be one of the twentieth century's finest novelists – but can you name five of his novels? 5 points for you if you can. There are twenty-six possible answers.

**Round 2, Part A) Awesome Alliteration** – I will give you the author and the year of publication. Name the alliterative title for a point:

11. Anna Sewell, 1877
12. Muriel Spark, 1959
13. Gillian Flynn, 2012
14. Thomas Mann, 1924
15. David Walliams, 2013

**Round 2, Part B) Blankety Books** – Find the missing word: there's always a theme and this quiz the theme is . . . parts of the body. A point for each one you get:

16. *[Blanks] and the Man* by George Bernard Shaw
17. *The Fourth [Blank]* by John Irving
18. *I Feel Bad About My [Blank] and Other Thoughts on Being a Woman* by Nora Ephron
19. *[Blank]smith* by Sarah Waters
20. *Cover Her [Blank]* by P. D. James

**Round 3, Part A) Two of a Kind** – I will describe a character and then an author. They share the same initials so, if you know one it will help you get the other. A point for each you can name:

21. Character: The young boy created by Jeff Brown in 1964 who is squashed flat by a bulletin board while he sleeps; he survives and then tries to make the best of being flat in a series of adventures; Brown wrote six books starring this character and other authors have since taken him on. Author: The comedian, writer and director who first appeared on television as part of a double act with Richard Herring; he has since had a successful solo career, including four series of his *Comedy Vehicle*; his books include *How I Escaped My Certain Fate – The Life and Deaths of a Stand-Up Comedian* and in 2019 *March of the Lemmings*.

22. Character: The 'American Psycho' himself from Bret Easton Ellis's 1991 novel, played in the film version by Christian Bale. Author: The author who was the first American to win the Man Booker Prize, for his 2016 novel *The Sellout*; his other novels include *Tuff*, *The White Boy Shuffle* and *Slumberland*.

23. Character: Noddy's friend and father figure in Toy Town, created by Enid Blyton; he is the only non-toy in Toyland. Author: The British author of the 2019 Man Booker Prize joint-winner *Girl, Woman, Other*; her other books include *Mr Loverman* and *Soul Tourists*.
24. Character: The girl with the dragon tattoo, created by Stieg Larsson in 2005 and whose later appearances include *The Girl Who Lived Twice* by David Lagercrantz. Author: The American author of young adult novels, best known for his 'Wayside School' series and *Holes* from 1998.
25. Character: Finally, the chief protagonist from Ray Bradbury's classic dystopian novel *Fahrenheit 451*; he works as a 'fireman', burning books and the buildings books are found in; in the 1966 film he was played by Oskar Werner and in the 2018 HBO version by Michael B. Jordan. Author: The American author of books for children and adults, who is best known for his 1995 novel *Wicked: The Life and Times of the Wicked Witch of the West*, based on characters created by L. Frank Baum in his 'Wizard of Oz' series; the book spawned the hugely successful musical *Wicked*.

**Round 3, Part B) BFG or BS?** Are these genuine words used by the BFG in Roald Dahl's 1982 book or ... not. BFG if they're Dahl, and BS if they are not:

26. Grotbaggling
27. Frothbuggling
28. Quogwinkle
29. Blimshazzled
30. Trogglehumper

**Round 4, Part A) RomeNo or JuliYes** – Are these genuine Shakespeare insults or made up by me? A point for each correctly identified insult. If you think it's genuine write or say JuliYes! If you think it's made up then it's RomeNo!

31. Thou pribbling weak kneed hedgehog
32. A weasel hath not such a deal of spleen as you are toss'd with
33. Your virginity breeds mites, much like a cheese
34. Why this swine hast fairer features than thy pestilent countenance
35. Thou art a boil, a plague sore, an embossed carbuncle, in my corrupted blood

**Round 4, Part B) Literature Links and Lists** – Answer these novel conundrums for a point each:

36. What links *The Road* by Cormac McCarthy, *The Ipcress File* by Len Deighton and *The Vanished* by Bill Pronzini?
37. Which award links Ann Leckie, Emily St John Mandel, Adrian Tchaikovsky and Colson Whitehead?
38. What links the author of *Three Men in a Boat*, the author of *Parade's End* and the male protagonist in Nabokov's *Lolita*?
39. Who comes next in this list: Severus Snape, Nagini, Bellatrix Lestrange . . .?
40. Name the link between Oscar Wilde, Boris Pasternak and Anna Sewell.

Finally, there are six 'SayWhatYouSee' visual representations of novels. Give yourself a point for the author and a point for the title.

Total up your answers and see how many you scored.
    The highest score possible on this quiz is 61.
    Thanks for playing!

3

4

# The Answers

1. C) *The Loneliness of the Long-distance Runner*, 1959 (*Born to Run* and *What I Talk About When I Talk About Running*, both 2007)
2. William Faulkner
3. B) *The Great Gatsby* by F. Scott Fitzgerald
4. Eric Morecambe
5. C) *Slugs* (that is a Shaun Hutson novel)
6. 'Old age should burn and rave at close of day'
7. A) He opened the first Saab dealership in America[*]
8. James Joyce
9. 1972
10. *The Man Within*, *The Name of Action* (repudiated by author, never republished), *Rumour at Nightfall* (repudiated by author, never republished), *Stamboul Train* (also published as *Orient Express*), *It's a Battlefield*, *England Made Me* (also published as *The Shipwrecked*), *A Gun for Sale* (also published as *This Gun for Hire*), *Brighton Rock*, *The Confidential Agent*, *The Power and the Glory* (also published as *The Labyrinthine Ways*),

[*] People have disputed that it was actually the first. It closed quite quickly and Vonnegut said (in an article published in 2004), 'The Saab then as now was a Swedish car, and I now believe my failure as a dealer so long ago explains what would otherwise remain a deep mystery: Why the Swedes have never given me a Nobel Prize for Literature.' Oh, and Barnes & Noble was founded in 1873.

*The Ministry of Fear, The Heart of the Matter, The Third Man* (novella), *The End of the Affair, The Quiet American, Loser Takes All, Our Man in Havana, A Burnt-out Case, The Comedians, Travels with My Aunt, The Honorary Consul, The Human Factor, Doctor Fischer of Geneva or The Bomb Party, Monsignor Quixote, The Tenth Man, The Captain and the Enemy*

11. *Black Beauty*
12. *Memento Mori*
13. *Gone Girl*
14. *The Magic Mountain*
15. *The Demon Dentist*
16. *Arms*
17. *Hand*
18. *Neck*
19. *Finger*
20. *Face*
21. Stanley Lambchop and Stewart Lee
22. Patrick Bateman and Paul Beatty
23. Big Ears and Bernardine Evaristo
24. Lisbeth Salander and Louis Sachar
25. Guy Montag and Gregory Maguire
26. BS
27. BFG – it means silly
28. BFG – it means great
29. BS
30. BFG – it means bad dream
31. RomeNo!
32. JuliYes! It's from *Henry IV, Part 1*
33. JuliYes! It's from *All's Well That Ends Well*
34. RomeNo!
35. JuliYes! It's from *King Lear*
36. The main characters are not named
37. They are all winners of the Arthur C. Clarke Award

38. They have the same first and last name: Jerome K. Jerome, Ford Maddox Ford and Humbert Humbert

39. Tom Riddle/Lord Voldemort – these are the final deaths in the final 'Harry Potter' novel, *The Deathly Hallows*, in order

40. They all wrote only one novel: Oscar Wilde, *The Picture of Dorian Gray*, Boris Pasternak, *Dr Zhivago*, Anna Sewell, *Black Beauty*

41. *The Shipping News* by Annie Proulx

42. *Toby's Room* by Pat Barker

43. *The Tears of the Giraffe* by Alexander McCall Smith

44. *The Man in the High Castle* by Philip K Dick

45. *The Dutch House* by Ann Patchett

46. *End of Watch* by Stephen King

# Quiz Number 16

**Round 1: This and that . . .** all the questions in this round are worth 1 point except question 10, which is worth 5.

1. **The First Question** – Which one of these Julia Donaldson characters appeared in print first: A) the Gruffalo, B) Stickman or C) Zog?

2. **Anagram** – The anagram is always an author's name: DERAILS HUMANS

3. **Book Quote** – Can you name the book from which this quote comes? 'It is an old maxim of mine that when you have excluded the impossible, whatever remains, however improbable, must be the truth.' Is it from: A) 'The Adventure of the Beryl Coronet' by Sir Arthur Conan Doyle, B) *The Crow Trap* by Ann Cleeves, C) *The Mysterious Affair at Styles* by Agatha Christie or D) *Mr Impossible* by Roger Hargreaves?

4. 'You would need to have a heart of stone not to laugh at the death of Little Nell' is a quote by which author?

5. **Odd One Out** – Which of the following is not a real Caitlin Moran book: A) *How to Build a Girl*, B) *How to Be Champion*, C) *How to Be Famous* or D) *How to Be a Woman*?

6. **Poetry Corner** – What is the next line? This quiz the poem is 'On the Ning Nang Nong' by Spike Milligan: 'On the Ning Nang Nong . . .'

7. **Fact or Fiction** – Which of the following is a fact about Hunter S. Thompson (actually it's about Hunter S.

Thompson's funeral): A) at Hunter's funeral his ashes were mixed with gasoline and poured into a Harley-Davidson's engine – the biker then drove to Las Vegas, B) at Hunter's funeral his ashes were mixed into marijuana-filled space cakes so the guests could get high on/with Hunter one last time or C) Hunter's ashes were fired from a cannon 47 metres in the air accompanied by red, white, blue and green fireworks?

8. This book was published in France in 1963. It was made into a hit film in 1968 – that hit lead to four sequels, and the series of films ended in 1973. The book was then turned into a TV series, which ran for one season in 1974 but was then cancelled. An animated version was made in 1975 but this too was cancelled after one season. A reimagining by Tim Burton was released in 2001. Most recently a new series of three films was produced, beginning in 2011 and ending in 2017. The enduring characters have also featured in computer games and graphic novels. Can you name the book?

9. **What Year?** – In which year did these literary events take place? If you're playing in teams give a point to whichever team gets nearest. Cecil Day-Lewis is announced as the new Poet Laureate. Alan Bennett's first stage play *Forty Years On* premieres in London's West End and the first non-Fleming Bond book is released (*Colonel Sun* by Kingsley Amis, under the name Robert Markham). Also published: *The Tiger Who Came to Tea* by Judith Kerr and *A Kestrel for a Knave* by Barry Hines. John Steinbeck passes away and this year sees the birth of Karl Ove Knausgård.

10. **Give Me Five** – This time it's Pulitzer Prize-winners from the twenty-first century that begin with the word 'The'. There are eight to guess – get five for 5 points!

**Round 2, Part A) Gandalf or Bruce Lee?** – Who said it? Attribute the quote to either Gandalf from *The Lord of the Rings* or martial arts legend Bruce Lee. A point if you are correct:

11. 'Death is just another path, one that we all must take.'
12. 'Knowledge will give you power, but character respect'
13. 'He that breaks a thing to find out what it is, has left the path of wisdom'
14. 'A wise man can learn more from a foolish question than a fool can learn from a wise answer'
15. 'It is wisdom to recognise necessity, when all other courses have been weighed, though as folly it may appear to those who cling to false hope'

**Round 2, Part B) Blankety Books** – Find the missing word: there's always a theme and this quiz the theme is . . . one-word Beatles songs. A point for each one you get:

16. *God [Blank] the Child* by Toni Morrison
17. *The [Blank] of Ink and Stars* by Keren Millwood Hargrave
18. *Sheltering [Blank]* by Jojo Moyes
19. *[Blank] to Live For* by Richard Roper
20. *Keep the Aspidistra [Blank]* by George Orwell

**Round 3, Part A) Two of a Kind** – I will describe a character and then an author. They share the same initials so if you know one it will help you get the other. A point for each you can name:

21. Character: The headmaster of Hogwarts in J. K. Rowling's 'Harry Potter' series; he is also revealed to be the founder and leader of the Order of the Phoenix

– the organisation opposed to Lord Voldemort and his plans; in the films he was portrayed by Richard Harris and then Michael Gambon. Author: The French author and playwright, born in 1802, who wrote such classics as *The Count of Monte Cristo* and *The Three Musketeers*.

22. Character: The apple of Adrian Mole's eyes in Sue Townsend's novels, this character first appears in *The Secret Diary of Adrian Mole, aged 13¾* in 1982; she and Adrian are an on–off couple until they finally split in *The True Confessions of Adrian Albert Mole* (1989); she was played by Lindsey Stagg, and later by Helen Baxendale. Author: The American author, screenwriter and ocean activist best known for his 1974 novel *Jaws* – he also co-wrote the screenplay; his other works include *The Deep*, *The Island* and *Beast*.

23. Character: Created by J. R. R. Tolkien, he is the leader of the company of dwarves who wish to reclaim the Lonely Mountain from Smaug the Dragon in the 1937 book *The Hobbit*; Bilbo Baggins joins the company as a thief. Author: Born in Serbia, now living in the USA, she is best known for *The Tiger's Wife*, which won the Orange Prize for Fiction in 2011; her second novel, *Inland*, was published in 2019.

24. Character: Mark Twain character that first appeared in *The Adventures of Tom Sawyer* and went on to feature in the title of the sequel. Author: The British novelist and screenwriter best known for creating 'Bridget Jones'.

25. Character : The detective inspector created by R. D. Wingfield in 1984; messy in his habits and personal life but a genius at solving mysteries, this character appeared in ten novels and was played by David Jason on television for eighteen years. Author: The British novelist whose first novel *The Eyre Affair* was published in 2001; best known for the 'Thursday Next' novels, he has a

unique style combining literary allusions, wordplay, parody and metafiction; his other works include *First Among Sequels* and *Shades of Grey*.

**Round 3, Part B) Initially Known as ...** – Authors known by their initials and their surname. I'll tell you what the initials stand for and give you their year of birth. Just tell me the surname for a point:

26. Pelham Grenville, 1881
27. Edward Estlin, 1894
28. Susan Eloise, 1948
29. Elwyn Brooks, 1899
30. Herbert George, 1866

**Round 4, Part A) Land Ho!** – I will give you the name of a ship that features in a book and the year of publication. Name the book and the author – a point for each:

31. *Nautilus*, 1870
32. *Hispaniola*, 1883
33. *Demeter*, 1897
34. SS *Nan-Shan*, 1902
35. *Pequod*, 1851

**Round 4, Part B) Literature Links and Lists** – Answer these novel conundrums for a point each.

36. Which New York borough (five to choose from!) links books by Hubert Selby Jr, Betty Smith and Jonathan Lethem?
37. What connects these picture books: *Hey Grandude!* (2019), *Mr Peabody's Apples* (2006) and *The Magically Mysterious Adventures of Noelle the Bulldog* (2005)?

38. What connects Ken Follett and Vitoria-Gasteiz (northern Spain), Hans Christian Andersen and New York's Central Park, and Oscar Wilde and Adelaide Street, Charing Cross, London?

39. What word connects the titles of a Bill Bryson book of 2019, the Stephen King novella on which the film *Stand by Me* was based and a famous Miss Marple mystery centred on the murder of Ruby Keene?

40. What is the number? How many titles are there in the (original) 'increasingly inaccurately named *Hitchhiker's Guide to the Galaxy* trilogy' by Douglas Adams? How many 'quarters of the orange' are there in Joanne Harris's novel of 2000? And what is the number in the title of the fourth book in Pittacus Lore's 'Lorien Legacies'?

Finally, there are six 'SayWhatYouSee' visual representations of novels. Give yourself a point for the author and a point for the title.

Total up your answers and see how many you scored.

The highest score possible on this quiz is 61.

Thanks for playing!

# The Answers

1. A) The Gruffalo, 1999 (Stickman, 2008, Zog, 2010)
2. Salman Rushdie
3. A) 'The Adventures of the Beryl Coronet' by Sir Arthur Conan Doyle*
4. Oscar Wilde
5. B) *How to Be Champion* (this is by Sarah Millican)
6. 'Where the Cows go Bong!'
7. C) Hunter's ashes were fired from a canon†
8. *Planet of the Apes* by Pierre Boulle
9. 1968
10. 2001: *The Amazing Adventures of Kavalier and Clay* by Michael Chabon; 2007: *The Road* by Cormac McCarthy; 2008: *The Brief Wondrous Life of Oscar Wao* by Junot Díaz; 2013: *The Orphan Master's Son* by Adam Johnson; 2014: *The Goldfinch* by Donna Tartt; 2016: *The Sympathizer* by Viet Thanh Nguyen; 2017: *The Underground Railroad* by Colson Whitehead; 2019: *The Overstory* by Richard Powers
11. Gandalf
12. Bruce Lee
13. Gandalf
14. Bruce Lee
15. Gandalf

---

* Sherlock Holmes of course; B) and C) are the debuts of Vera Stanhope and Hercule Poirot respectively.
† The Funeral cost $3 million and was paid for by Johnny Depp. The music playing was Norman Greenbaum, 'Spirit in the Sky'.

16. *Help*
17. *Girl*
18. *Rain*
19. *Something*
20. *Flying*
21. Albus Dumbledore and Alexander Dumas*
22. Pandora Braithwaite and Peter Benchley
23. Thorin Oakenshield and Téa Obreht
24. Huckleberry Finn and Helen Fielding
25. Jack Frost and Jasper Fforde
26. P. G. Wodehouse
27. e. e. cummings
28. S. E. Hinton
29. E. B. White
30. H. G. Wells
31. *Twenty Thousand Leagues Under the Sea* by Jules Verne
32. *Treasure Island* by Robert Louis Stevenson
33. *Dracula* by Bram Stoker
34. *Typhoon* by Joseph Conrad
35. *Moby Dick* by Herman Melville
36. Brooklyn: Hubert Selby Jr, *Last Exit to Brooklyn*, Betty Smith, *A Tree Grows in Brooklyn*, Jonathan Lethem, *Motherless Brooklyn*
37. They are all by singers: *Hey Grandude!* by Paul McCartney, *Mr Peabody's Apples* by Madonna, *The Magically Mysterious Adventures of Noelle the Bulldog* by Gloria Estefan
38. There are statues of the authors in those places
39. Body: both the Bryson and King books are called *The Body*, and Christie's is called *The Body in the Library*

* Among his many honours and tributes Dumas has a Paris Métro station named after him and you can visit a museum at his previous address, the Château de Monte-Cristo.

40. Five: five books in Adams's 'trilogy', *Five Quarters of the Orange* and *The Fall of Five*
41. *The Owl Service* by Alan Garner
42. *Walking on Glass* by Iain Banks
43. *Ringworld* by Larry Niven
44. *The Old Curiosity Shop* by Charles Dickens
45. *Catch 22* by Joseph Heller
46. *Accordion Crimes* by Annie Proulx

# Quiz Number 17

**Round 1: This and That** . . . all the questions in this round are worth 1 point except question 10, which is worth 5.

1. **The First Question** – Which of these Harry Potter Books has the highest word count: A) *Harry Potter and the Philosopher's Stone*, B) *Harry Potter and the Goblet of Fire* or C) *Harry Potter and the Half-Blood Prince*?

2. **Anagram** – The anagram is always an author's name: MAINLY LATHER

3. **Book Quote** – Can you name the book from which this quote comes? 'Sometimes human places, create inhuman monsters.' Is it from: A) *A Monster Calls* by Patrick Ness, B) *The Shining* by Stephen King, C) *One Flew Over the Cuckoo's Nest* by Ken Kesey or D) *The Dirt: Confessions of the World's Most Notorious Rock Band* by Mötley Crüe?

4. Which much loved character created by A. A. Milne doesn't get introduced until his second book about Winnie-the-Pooh?

5. **Odd One Out** – As well as many well-respected novels, Tom Wolfe wrote thirteen non-fiction books in all. Here are four titles, but one isn't genuine. Is it: A) *The Electric Kool-Aid Acid Test*, B) *My Friend Jack Eats Sugar Lumps*, C) *The Kandy-Kolored Tangerine-Flake Streamline Baby* or D) *Radical Chic & Mau-Mauing the Flak Catchers*?

6. **Poetry Corner** – What is the next line? This quiz the poem is 'Do Not Stand at My Grave and Weep' by Mary Elizabeth Frye: 'Do not stand at my grave and weep . . .'

7. **Fact or Fiction** – Which of the following is a fact about Ian Rankin: A) Ian Rankin keeps two pigs called Snowball and Napoleon on his farm in Edinburgh, B) as a teenage punk he was in a band called the Dancing Pigs or C) Ian Rankin has a 'Porky Pig' tattoo on his calf that he had done while drunk?

8. Which literary character, who first appeared in 1887, was originally called 'Ormond Sacker'?

9. **What year?** – In which year did these literary events take place? If you're playing in teams give a point to whichever team gets nearest. Published this year: Tony Parsons's *Man and Boy*, Joanne Harris's *Chocolat* and J. K. Rowling's *Harry Potter and the Prisoner of Azkaban*. Iris Murdoch dies as does *Godfather* author Mario Puzo. Stephen King gets hit by a van and is in hospital for three weeks, and Andrew Motion is appointed Poet Laureate.

10. **Give Me Five** – Virginia Woolf wrote ten novels. Can you name five? There's a point for each one you know.

**Round 2, Part A) Poop Poop!** – Cars in literature, a point per question:

11. Which car-loving character in Kenneth Grahame's *The Wind in the Willows* (having been asked to promise never to touch a motor car again) declares 'Certainly not! ... On the contrary, I faithfully promise that the very first motor-car I see, poop-poop! off I go in it!'

12. Who is the author of *Drive*, the 2005 novel that was filmed in 2011 starring Ryan Gosling?

13. Who wrote the book *Chitty-Chitty-Bang-Bang*? For a bonus point, which famous author co-wrote the screenplay?

14. What type of car is used by Ron and Harry in the 'Harry Potter' series?

15. What is the name of the car in Stephen King's 1983 novel that stars a 1958 Plymouth Fury?

**Round 2, Part B) Blankety Books** – Find the missing word: there's always a theme and this quiz the theme is ... characters (i.e. colours) from *Reservoir Dogs*. A point for each one you get:

16. *How Hitler Stole [Blank] Rabbit* by Judith Kerr
17. *The Concrete [Blank]* by Michael Connelly
18. *Straight [Blank] Male* by John Niven
19. *Porterhouse [Blank]* by Tom Sharpe
20. *The [Blank] Girl* by Jostein Gaarder

**Round 3, Part A) Two of a Kind** – I will describe a character and then an author. They share the same initials so if you know one it will help you get the other. A point for each one you can name:

21. Character: This 'Harry Potter' character is a student in the Slytherin house and the son of Lucius and Narcissa. Author: The English author of the Man Booker Prize-shortlisted *Cloud Atlas*, *The Bone Clocks* and, in 2020, *Utopia Avenue*.

22. Character: The name of the professor created by Dan Brown who appears in *The Da Vinci Code*, *Angels and Demons* and more; he is played in the film versions by Tom Hanks; he is a professor of the history of art and 'symbology' at Harvard University. Author: The author that created Jason Bourne in the Bourne series, which has been carried on by others since his death in 2001 and is still hugely successful.

23. Character: The main character from the first half of John Steinbeck's *East of Eden*, he is the son of Cyrus and the father of Aron and Cal; he falls in love with the

evil Cathy Ames. Author: The American author perhaps best known for her debut novel, 1989's *The Joy Luck Club*, which was filmed in 1993.

24. Character: The cruel, one-eyed, Yorkshire schoolmaster who runs Dotheboys Hall – the boarding school in *Nicholas Nickleby* by Charles Dickens. Author: The British international bestselling author who specialises in historical fiction set in southern Africa; his bestsellers include *Shout at the Devil*, *River God* and *The Triumph of the Sun*.

25. Character: Finally, the character created by Roald Dahl who releases five golden tickets that grant entry into his mysterious chocolate factory. Author: The great English romantic poet born in 1770 who Coleridge helped to launch the Romantic Age with their joint publication *Lyrical Ballads* in 1798; he was Poet Laureate from 1843 until his death in 1850; he is perhaps best known for his poem 'I wandered lonely as a cloud' aka 'Daffodils'.

**Round 3, Part B) Money Money Money** – Five questions involving books and money! A point per question to be won:

26. From 2002 to 2013 *Forbes* published a fictional top 15 rich list – which J. R. R. Tolkien character was second in the final one?

27. One of the most famous literary misers – name the titular character of George Eliot's third novel.

28. In 2007 former stockbroker and trader Jordan Belfort published his bestselling autobiography – what was it called?

29. In 2017 Jane Austen replaced Charles Darwin on the £10 note – but which author had Darwin replaced?

30. What is the name of Michael Lewis's bestseller about baseball from 2004?

**Round 4, Part A) Tales of the Cities** – All these books have cities in the title. I will give you the year of publication, the author and the country the city is in. You tell me the book's title for a point:

31. 1989, Martin Amis, England
32. 2002, Åsne Seierstad, Afghanistan
33. 2013, Nina George, France
34. 2006, C. J. Sansom, Spain
35. 1939, Christopher Isherwood, Germany

**Round 4, Part B) Literature Links and Lists** – Answer these novel conundrums for a point each:

36. What is the link between *The Man in the High Castle* by Philip K Dick, *SS-GB* by Len Deighton and *Fatherland* by Robert Harris?
37. What word connects books in series by Cassandra Clare, Louise Hare and Jeanne DuPrau?
38. Which sport features in the books *The Art of Fielding* by Chad Harbach, *Shoeless Joe* by W. P. Kinsella, *The Girl Who Loved Tom Gordon* by Stephen King and *The Natural* by Bernard Malamud?
39. What connects the characters: Harry Potter, Huckleberry Finn, Alex Rider and Jane Eyre?
40. What preserve connects Paddington Bear and the character created by Andrew Davies – played on TV by Charlotte Coleman?

Finally, there are six 'SayWhatYouSee' visual representations of novels. Give yourself a point for the author and a point for the title.

Total up your answers and see how many you scored.
    The highest score possible on this quiz is 62.
    Thanks for playing!

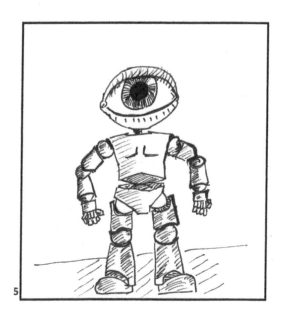

# The Answers

1. B) *Harry Potter and the Goblet of Fire*\*
2. Hilary Mantel
3. B) *The Shining* by Stephen King
4. Tigger
5. B) *My Friend Jack Eats Sugarlumps* (this is a lyric from the song 'My Friend Jack' by The Smoke)
6. 'I am not there. I do not sleep.'
7. B) He was in a punk band called the Dancing Pigs
8. Dr John Watson
9. 1999
10. *Between the Acts, Flush: A Biography, Jacob's Room, Mrs Dalloway, Night and Day, Orlando: A Biography, To the Lighthouse, The Voyage Out, The Waves, The Years*
11. Mr Toad
12. James Sallis
13. Ian Fleming; Roald Dahl co-wrote the screenplay
14. A (flying) Ford Anglia
15. Christine
16. *Pink*
17. *Blonde*
18. *White*
19. *Blue*
20. *Orange*
21. Draco Malfoy and David Mitchell

\* That has 190,637 words, *Half-Blood Prince* has 168,923 and *Philosopher's Stone* has 76,944, according to Fostergrant.co.uk.

22. Robert Langdon and Robert Ludlum
23. Adam Trask and Amy Tan
24. Wackford Squeers and Wilbur Smith
25. Willy Wonka and William Wordsworth
26. Smaug with $54.1 billion; the source of his wealth was 'marauding'*
27. Silas Marner
28. *The Wolf of Wall Street*
29. Charles Dickens
30. *Moneyball: The Art of Winning an Unfair Game*
31. *London Fields*
32. *The Bookseller of Kabul*
33. *The Little Paris Bookshop*
34. *Winter in Madrid*
35. *Goodbye to Berlin*
36. They are 'alternative history' books in which Germany didn't lose the Second World War
37. City: *City of Bones* by Cassandra Clare, *This Lovely City* by Louise Hare, *The City of Ember* by Jeanne DuPrau
38. Baseball†
39. They are all orphans
40. Marmalade (Coleman played Marmalade Atkins)
41. *The Amazing Adventures of Kavalier and Clay* by Michael Chabon
42. *The Moon's a Balloon* by David Niven
43. *The Buried Giant* by Kazuo Ishiguro
44. *The Remorseful Day* by Colin Dexter
45. *I Robot* by Isaac Asimov
46. *The Closed Circle* by Jonathan Coe

* Scrooge McDuck was first with a grand total of $64.5 billion, source: mining, treasure hunting.
† *Shoeless Joe* is the book that became the film *Field of Dreams*.

# Quiz Number 18

**Round 1: This and That . . .** all the questions in this round are worth 1 point except question 10, which is worth 5.

1. **The First Question** –Which of these was published first: A) *The Song of Achilles* by Madeline Miller, B) *Song of Solomon* by Toni Morrison or C) *A Song of Shadows* by John Connolly?
2. **Anagram** – The anagram is always an author's name: TEACUP MATRON
3. **Book Quote** – Can you name the book from which book this quote comes? 'Deep in the human unconscious is a pervasive need for a logical universe that makes sense. But the real universe is always one step beyond logic.' Is it from: A) *Dune* by Frank Herbert, B) *2001: A Space Odyssey* by Arthur C Clarke, C) *The God Delusion* by Richard Hawkins or D) *The World According to Danny Dyer* by Danny Dyer?
4. In Cervantes's seventeenth-century masterpiece *Don Quixote*, what is the name of Don Quixote's squire?
5. **Odd One Out** – Which of the following is not a real Jeffrey Archer novel: A) *Honour Among Thieves*, B) *The Sins of the Father*, C) *Pop Goes the Weasel* or D) *Not a Penny More, Not a Penny Less*?
6. **Poetry Corner** – What is the next line? This quiz the poem is 'Still I Rise' by Maya Angelou: 'You may write me down in history/With your bitter, twisted lies . . .'
7. **Fact or Fiction** –Which of the following is a fact about *Cloud Atlas* author David Mitchell: A) not only does

David Mitchell have the same name as the comedian he also shares his birthday, B) David Mitchell wrote a book in 2016 that won't be read by anyone for a 100 years as part of a conservation programme in Oslo or C) David Mitchell served ten months in prison in 1998 after being convicted of robbing 1980s singer Paul Young's flat?

8. This book was published in 1911 (after being serialised in the *American Magazine*) and has been adapted many times. First published in America but set in Yorkshire, the first film was produced in 1919 – though no print has survived. Another version followed in 1949 and then another in 1993 starring Maggie Smith. There is also a new version starring Julie Walters and Colin Firth. There have been TV versions, and very successful stage versions. What is the title?

9. **What year?** – In which year did these literary events take place? If you're playing in teams give a point to whichever team gets nearest. Published this year: *Harry Potter and the Order of the Phoenix*, Lynn Truss's *Eats, Shoots & Leaves* and Khaled Hosseini's *The Kite Runner*. Roberto Bolaño and Carol Shields both pass away. D. B. C. Pierre wins the Booker with *Vernon God Little* and in the cinema the highest grossing film is *The Lord of the Rings: The Return of the King*.

10. **Give Me Five** – Ernest Hemingway wrote ten novels and novellas (not including story collections or non-fiction). Can you name five for 5 points?

**Round 2, Part A) READ** – Five one-word book titles that start with R E A or D. I'll give you the author and the year of publication, and you give me the title for a point:

11. Chimamanda Ngozi Adichie, 2013
12. Stephenie Meyer, 2007

13. J. M. Coetzee, 1999
14. Ian McEwan, 2001
15. Daphne du Maurier, 1938

**Round 2, Part B) Blankety Books** – Find the missing word: there's always a theme and this quiz the theme is . . . the Moon and spaceflight. A point for each one you get:

16. *[Blank] Park* by Bret Easton Ellis
17. *[Blank] Strike* by Anthony Horowitz
18. *Station [Blank]* by Emily St John Mandel
19. *The Girl on the [Blank]* by Paul Torday
20. *A Closed and Common [Blank]* by Becky Chambers

**Round 3, Part A) Two of a Kind** – I will describe a character and then an author. They share the same initials so if you know one it will help you get the other. A point for each you can name:

21. Character: Susanna Clarke creation who shares the title of her 2004 novel with 'Mr Norrell'; he was played in the TV adaptation by Bertie Carvel. Author: The American author, born in 1902, of *The Grapes of Wrath* and *Of Mice and Men*; he won the Nobel Prize in Literature in 1962.

22. Character: The Charles Dickens character, a retired businessman, who appears in the title of his first novel from 1836. Author: The writer of Waterstones' 2016 Book of the Year *The Essex Serpent*, *After Me Comes the Flood* and *Melmoth*.

23. Character: The character at the centre of a Stephen King novel from 1977 who takes his family to the Overlook Hotel in Colorado, which he has been employed to maintain over the winter; there he is haunted by the ghosts of

the hotel. Author: The Scottish author and playwright, born in 1896, best known for her mystery novels, especially the 'Inspector Alan Grant' series.

24. Character: The main protagonist of the 'Vampire Academy' series created by Richelle Mead; beginning in 2008, this series of six books has sold over 8 million copies; the first book (*Vampire Academy*) was filmed in 2014. Author: The English bestselling author best known for his works of historical fiction such as *Fatherland*, *Enigma* and *Archangel*; he also wrote the screenplay for the 2010 film *The Ghost Writer*.

25. Character: And finally, the titular character from the 2019 hit by Taylor Jenkins Reid; the character is a rock star with her band The Six and the novel deals with the band's whirlwind rise and infamous break up. Author: The German-born American author best known for his 1992 collection of short stories *Jesus' Son*, his novel *Tree of Smoke* (2007) and his 2011 novella *Train Dreams*.

**Round 3, Part B) Well played** – Sports autobiographies. I'll give you the name of the book, the initials of the author and the year of publication: just tell me the author's name.

26. *Open*, AA, 2009
27. *My Life in Football*, KK, 2018
28. *Proud: My Autobiography*, GT, 2014
29. *Taking on the World*, EM, 2002
30. *No Spin: My Autobiography*, SW, 2018

**Round 4, Part A) Oh, and Thingy … Whatsit …** Name the missing member of these groups for a point:

31. So far, there are five books in George R. R. Martin's 'Song of Ice and Fire': *A Game of Thrones*, *A Clash of*

*Kings, A Storm of Swords, A Dance with Dragons* and which other?

32. In Arthur Ransome's *Swallows and Amazons*, there are five Walkers who crew the *Swallow* (so not including Mary the mum) but which one is missing: Susan, Roger, Bridget aka Vicky, Titty . . .?

33. Name the missing book from James Ellroy's 'LA Quartet': *White Jazz, The Big Nowhere, The Black Dahlia* and . . .?

34. There are five Bennet sisters from Jane Austen's *Pride and Prejudice*: Elizabeth, Mary, Catherine aka 'Kitty', Lydia and which other?

35. There are four named positions in Quidditch: Chasers, Beaters, Keeper and which other?

**Round 4, Part B) Literature Links and Lists** – Answer these novel conundrums for a point each:

36. Which is the odd one out of these 3 pairs: A) Martin and Kingsley Amis, B) Evelyn and Auberon Waugh and C) Gerald and Lawrence Durrell?

37. What flower and girl's name appears in the titles of books by Henry James and in a series for children by Kes Gray, and is the female protagonist in *The Great Gatsby* by F. Scott Fitzgerald?

38. What comes next in this list: *Inheritance* (2011), *Brisingr* (2008), *Eldest* (2005) . . .?

39. What links Henry Miller's two books that begin with the word 'Tropic', Gavin G. Smith's 2012 sci-fi trilogy starter and the autobiography, titled called *Say Goodnight JV*, of an ex-snooker player and *Big Break* star?

40. What links J. M. Coetzee, Peter Carey, Hilary Mantel and Margaret Atwood?

Finally, there are six 'SayWhatYouSee' visual representations of novels. Give yourself a point for the author and a point for the title.

Total up your answers and see how many you scored.

The highest score possible on this quiz is 61.

Thanks for playing!

# The Answers

1. B) *Song of Solomon*, 1977 (*The Song of Achilles*, 2011, *A Song of Shadows*, 2015)
2. Truman Capote
3. A) *Dune* by Frank Herbert
4. Sancho Panza
5. C) *Pop Goes the Weasel* (this is a James Patterson book)
6. 'You may trod me in the very dirt/But still, like dust, I'll rise'
7. B) He wrote a book in 2016 that won't be read by anyone for 100 years*
8. *The Secret Garden* by Frances Hodgson Burnett
9. 2003
10. *The Torrents of Spring, The Sun Also Rises, A Farewell to Arms, To Have and Have Not, For Whom the Bell Tolls, Across the River and into the Trees, The Old Man and the Sea, Islands in the Stream, The Garden of Eden, True at First Light*
11. *Americanah*

* This was as part of the Future Library Project where 1,000 trees were planted two years ago in Oslo's Nordmarka forest. Starting with Margaret Atwood, each year for the next 100 years an author will deliver a piece of writing that will only be read in 2114, when the trees are chopped down to make paper on which the 100 texts will be printed. Mitchell said the book was now 'as gone from me as a coin dropped in a river'. And if C) sounds familiar – that was TV Chef Gino D'Acampo.

12. *Eclipse*
13. *Disgrace*
14. *Atonement* (*Amsterdam* was 1998)
15. *Rebecca*
16. *Lunar*
17. *Eagle* (name of a lunar module)
18. *Eleven* (Apollo)
19. *Landing*
20. *Orbit*
21. Jonathan Strange and John Steinbeck
22. Samuel Pickwick and Sarah Perry
23. Jack Torrance and Josephine Tey (real name Elizabeth MacKintosh)
24. Rosemarie Hathaway and Robert Harris
25. Daisy Jones and Denis Johnson
26. Andre Agassi
27. Kevin Keegan
28. Gareth Thomas
29. Ellen MacArthur
30. Shane Warne
31. *A Feast for Crows*
32. John (eldest and captain)*
33. *LA Confidential*
34. Jane (eldest)
35. Seeker
36. C) Gerald and Lawrence Durrell are brothers: the others are father and son
37. Daisy
38. *Eragon*: this is the Christopher Paolini 'Inheritance' cycle in reverse publication order

* Titty's name was changed to Kitty for the 1963 BBC version and Tatty for another adaptation in 2016. The family of the woman who inspired the original Titty were furious.

39. Signs of the Zodiac: *Tropic of Cancer*, *Tropic of Capricorn*, *Age of Scorpio* and John Virgo

40. They have all won the Man Booker Prize twice.

41. *Mystic River* by Dennis Lehane

42. *A Wild Sheep Chase* by Haruki Murakami

43. *A Room with a View* by E.M. Forster

44. *A Kestrel for a Knave* by Barry Hines

45. *Pale Fire* (Pail fire) by Vladimir Nabakov

46. *Rabbit at Rest* by John Updike

# Quiz Number 19

**Round 1: This and That . . .** all the questions in this round are worth 1 point except question 10, which is worth 5.

1. **The First Question** – Which of these children's fantasy classics was published first: A) C. S. Lewis's *The Lion, the Witch and the Wardrobe*, B) J. R. R. Tolkien's *The Hobbit* or C) Alan Garner's *The Weirdstone of Brisingamen: A Tale of Alderley*?

2. **Anagram** – The anagram is always an author's name: AMORAL BLANK MICE

3. **Book Quote** – Can you name the book from which this quote comes? 'Heaven knows we need never be ashamed of our tears, for they are rain upon the blinding dust of earth.' Is it from: A) *Love in the Time of Cholera* by Gabriel García Márquez, B) *Great Expectations* by Charles Dickens, C) *The God of Small Things* by Arundhati Roy or D) *The Life of Rylan* by Rylan Clark-Neal?

4. What is the name given to the group of associated English writers, intellectuals, philosophers and artists in the first half of the twentieth century that included Virginia Woolf and E. M. Forster? The name of the group is derived from the area in London they all lived in or near.

5. **Odd One Out** – Which of the following is not a real Inspector Frost book by R. D. Wingfield: A) *Before the Frost*, B) *Night Frost*, C) *Hard Frost* or D) *A Killing Frost*?

6. **Poetry Corner** – What is the next line? This quiz the poem is 'Anthem for Doomed Youth' by Wilfred Owen: 'What passing-bells for these who die as cattle? . . .'

7. **Fact or Fiction** – Which of the following is a fact about Dr Seuss: A) Dr Seuss invented the word 'zany', B) Dr Seuss invented the word 'galumph' or C) Dr Seuss invented the word 'nerd'?

8. Which literary character's cat is immortalised in a monument on London's Highgate Hill?

9. **What year?** – In which year did these literary events take place? If you're playing in teams give a point to whichever team gets nearest. Charlotte Brontë would have been 200 this year! Published this year: *The Underground Railroad* by Colson Whitehead, *Days Without End* by Sebastian Barry and *The Essex Serpent* by Sarah Perry. Paul Beatty wins the Booker for *The Sellout* and is the first American to do so. *Watership Down* author Richard Adams passes away at age ninety-six and Dario Fo dies aged ninety.

10. **Give Me Five** – Name five of the creatures that James meets in Roald Dahl's *James and the Giant Peach* for 5 points. There are seven possible answers.

**Round 2, Part A) Book Bingo!** Get your Mecca daubers out! A point for every correct number you spot:

11. How many steps are there in the title of John Buchan's book of 1915: Rise and Shine 29, Will You Be Mine 39, PC 49 or Brighton Line 59?

12. How many 'Wizard of Oz' books did L. Frank Baum write: One Little Duck number 2, Tom Mix number 6, Valentine's Day number 14 or Jump and Jive 35?

13. How many streets are there in the title of the Catherine Cookson novel of 1952: Boris's Den number 10, Too

Shy to Be Seen number 15, Key of the Door 21 or In a State 28?

14. How many gables did the house have in Nathaniel Hawthorne's classic book of 1851: Cup of Tea number 3, Man Alive number 5, Lucky number 7 or One Dozen number 12?

15. What number is the dream in David Mitchell's book of 2001: Kelly's Eye number 1, Doctor's Orders number 9, Dancing Queen 17 or Duck and Dive 25?

**Round 2, Part B) Blankety Books** – Find the missing word: there's always a theme and this quiz the theme is . . . one-word sitcom titles. A point for each one you get:

16. *Three [Blanks] Secret Seven* by Enid Blyton
17. *A Spy Among [Blanks]* by Ben Macintyre
18. *Giant's [Blank]* by Mary Westmacott (Agatha Christie)
19. *Agatha Raisin and the [Blank] Vet* by M. C. Beaton
20. *Say You're [Blank]* by Karen Rose

**Round 3, Part A) Two of a Kind** – I will describe a character and then an author. They share the same initials so if you know one it will help you get the other. A point for each you can name:

21. Character: The titular character from Stuart Turton's popular 2018 Costa First Novel Award winner, in which she suffers 'seven deaths' ('seven and a half deaths' in the US). Author: The American author known as 'Papa'; hugely influential he wrote in a punchy economical style; he served as an ambulance driver in Italy during the First World War (after being turned down by the US military due to poor eyesight); his best-known works include *The Old Man and the Sea* and *A Farewell to Arms*.

22. Character: The 'holistic detective' created by Douglas Adams; he appeared in two novels, *The Long Dark Tea-time of the Soul* being the second; he has been portrayed on the screen by Stephen Mangan and Samuel Barnett, and on the radio by Harry Enfield. Author: The Israeli author who won the International Booker Prize in 2017 for his novel *A Horse Walks Into a Bar* and in 2018 he was awarded the Israel Prize for Literature.

23. Character: The eldest of the four siblings in C. S. Lewis's 'The Chronicles of Narnia' series, this character appears in four of the seven books. Author: The Oxford-based author of the fantasy trilogies 'His Dark Materials' and 'The Book of Dust'.

24. Character: The eldest sister from Diana Wynne Jones 1986 novel *Howl's Moving Castle*, she is turned into an old woman and becomes a cleaning lady in Howl's castle in the hope he may be able to remove the curse; the book was adapted as an animated film by Studio Ghibli in 2004. Author: The American author and essayist probably best known for her 2003 novel *What I Loved* and, from 2011, *The Summer Without Men*.

25. Character: Finally, the name of the lawyer from Harper Lee's *To Kill a Mockingbird*, played in the 1962 film by Gregory Peck. Author: Arguably the most famous diarist in history who tragically died in 1945.

**Round 3, Part B) No Wait, I Have a Better Idea . . . !**
– Everyone is allowed to change their mind and authors are no exception. Below I've listed the provisional title a book and the year it was published. Name the title under which the book was published for a point and the author for another.

26. 'First Impressions', 1813
27. 'The God of Illusions', 1992

28. 'Offred', 1985
29. 'All's Well that Ends Well', 1869
30. 'On the Road to West Egg', 1925

**Round 4, Part A) Books in the Movies** – A point for each correct answer:

31. Elmore Leonard's 1990 novel about mobsters in Hollywood was turned into a 1995 film starring John Travolta and more recently a US TV series – what is it called?
32. Which writer was played by Philip Seymour Hoffman and also by Toby Jones in two separate films released in the same year (in the UK)?
33. In 1987 which Hollywood actress released the semi-autobiographical bestseller *Postcards from the Edge*?
34. Which 1987 film adapted from his own novel by William Goldman begins with a grandfather reading to his poorly grandson and includes the line, 'When I was your age, television was called books'?
35. The 2018 film *All is True* featuring Kenneth Branagh and Judi Dench is about which playwright and poet?

**Round 4, Part B) Literature Links and Lists** – Answer these novel conundrums for a point each:

36. Which English county is the setting for *The Railway Children* by Edith Nesbit, *Behind the Scenes at the Museum* by Kate Atkinson and *The Damned United* by David Peace?
37. What is the link between C. S. Lewis, Clive Hamilton and N. W. Clerk?
38. What comes next in this list: *The Miserable Mill*, *The Wide Window*, *The Reptile Room* . . .?

39. What is the link between *What Dream May Come* by Richard Matheson, *Band of Brothers* by Stephen E. Ambrose and *Infinite Jest* by David Foster Wallace?

40. Which colour appears in the titles of books by Sebastian Faulks, Richard Llewelyn and Anne Enright?

Finally, there are six 'SayWhatYouSee' visual representations of novels. Give yourself a point for the author and a point for the title.

Total up your answers and see how many you scored.

The highest score possible on this quiz is 66.

Thanks for playing!

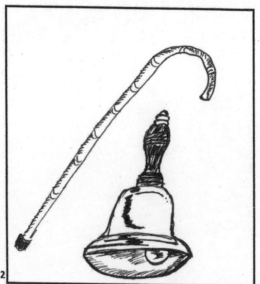

# The Answers

1. B) *The Hobbit*, 1937 (*The Lion, the Witch and the Wardrobe*, 1950, *The Weirdstone of Brisingamen*, 1960)
2. Malorie Blackman
3. B) *Great Expectations* by Charles Dickens
4. Bloomsbury group (or set)
5. A) *Before the Frost* (this is a Linda Wallander novel by Henning Mankell)
6. 'Only the monstrous anger of the guns'
7. C) Dr Seuss invented the word 'nerd'*
8. Dick Whittington
9. 2016†
10. The Centipede, the Earthworm, the Old Green Grasshopper, the Ladybug (Ladybird), Miss Spider, the Glowworm, the Silkworm
11. 39: *The Thirty-nine Steps*‡
12. 14
13. 15: *The Fifteen Streets*
14. 7: *The House of Seven Gables*

* The word 'nerd' was first seen in Dr Seuss's 1950 book *If I Ran the Zoo*. Many believe Shakespeare created the word 'zany' while the word 'galumph' sprang from the mind of Lewis Carroll.
† Richard Adams didn't publish his first book (*Watership Down*) until he was fifty-two. It was turned down by four publishers but once published (in 1972) was a huge success. The nightmare-inducing (but marvellous) film followed in 1978.
‡ I had to invent 'will you be mine', as the actual bingo call is 'Steps' . . . bit of a giveaway.

15. 9: *Number9Dream*
16. *Cheers*
17. *Friends*
18. *Bread*
19. *Vicious*
20. *Sorry*
21. Evelyn Hardcastle and Ernest Hemingway
22. Dirk Gently and David Grossman
23. Peter Pevensie and Philip Pullman
24. Sophie Hatter and Siri Hustvedt
25. Atticus Finch and Anne Frank
26. *Pride and Prejudice* by Jane Austen
27. *The Secret History* by Donna Tartt
28. *The Handmaid's Tale* – Margaret Atwood
29. *War and Peace* by Leo Tolstoy
30. *The Great Gatsby* by F. Scott Fitzgerald
31. *Get Shorty*
32. Truman Capote (*Capote* and *Infamous*, 2006)
33. Carrie Fisher
34. *The Princess Bride*
35. William Shakespeare
36. Yorkshire
37. They are all the same person*
38. *The Bad Beginning*: they are Lemony Snicket's 'A Series of Unfortunate Events' in reverse publication order
39. They all have titles taken from lines in Shakespeare plays: *Band of Brothers* is from *Henry V*, *What Dreams May Come* and *Infinite Jest* are from *Hamlet*
40. Green: *On Green Dolphin Street* by Sebastian Faulks, *How Green Was My Valley* by Richard Llewelyn, *The Green Road* by Anne Enright

* C. S. Lewis used the other two names: Clive Hamilton for poetry and N. W. Clerk for *A Grief Observed* about the death of his wife.

41. *Lucky Jim* (Lucky gym) by Kingsley Amis
42. *Kain and Abel* (Cane and a bell) by Jeffrey Archer
43. *Wild Swans* (Oscar Wilde swans) by Jung Chang
44. *The Ghost Road* (Ghost rode) by Pat Barker
45. *We Have Always Lived in the Castle* by Shirley Jackson
46. *A Clockwork Orange* by Anthony Burgess

# Quiz Number 20

**Round 1, This and That** . . . all the questions in this round are worth 1 point except question 10, which is worth 5.

1. **The First Question** – Which of these 'Misters' was published first: A) *Mr Nice* by Howard Marks, B) *Mr Loverman* by Bernardine Evaristo or C) *Mr Unbelievable* by Chris Kamara?

2. **Anagram** – The anagram is always an author's name: ACTION REALM

3. **Book Quote** – Can you name the book from which this quote comes? 'It is never too late to be wise.' Is it from: A) *The Hobbit* by J. R. R. Tolkien, B) *The Wind-up Bird Chronicle* by Haruki Murakami, C) *Robinson Crusoe* by Daniel Defoe or D) *Dennis Wise: The Autobiography* by Dennis Wise?

4. Who is the only author to have been both shortlisted for the Booker Prize and to have appeared as Ken Barlow's girlfriend in *Coronation Street*?

5. **Odd One Out** – Which of the following is not a real Ian Rankin book: A) *Let it Bleed*, B) *Revolver*, C) *Beggars Banquet* or D) *Black and Blue*?

6. **Poetry Corner** – What is the next line? This quiz the poem is 'To a Mouse' by Robert Burns: 'Wee, sleeket, cowran, tim'rous beastie . . .'

7. **Fact or Fiction** – Which of the following is a fact about Daniel Defoe: A) throughout his life Defoe was often in debt so one of his schemes to make money was to import

1,000 boomerangs from Australia in an attempt to make them a craze; sadly for Defoe the ship with his cargo sank in the Indian Ocean, B) in an attempt to escape his debts, Defoe bought a number of civets, which produce a scent (from a pouch under the tail) that is highly prized; sadly for Defoe before he could procure the scent his civets were seized by sheriffs in lieu of payment or C) to try and make some much-needed capital, Defoe attempted to convince his good friend and *Tristram Shandy* author Laurence Sterne to tour the theatres performing their works; sadly for Defoe his friend demurred due to his intense shyness?

8. This book, published in 1934, was the first in a series of eight books, the final one of which was published in 1988. It was filmed in 1964 and was a huge success, which makes the fact that a sequel film wasn't made until 2018 quite surprising. That distance of fifty-four years makes it the longest gap in history between live-action sequels. The book has also been made into a musical for the stage, first in 2004 and again in 2019. And in 2010 BBC Radio 7 broadcast a dramatisation starring Juliet Stevenson. Can you name the book?

9. **What year?** – In which year did these literary events take place? If you're playing in teams give a point to whichever team gets nearest. This year the first 'Goosebumps' book by R. L. Stine is published. along with P. D. James's *The Children of Men* and Iain Banks's *The Crow Road*. Isaac Asimov and Richard Yates both pass away. Michael Ondaatje and Barry Unsworth are joint winners of the Booker Prize with *The English Patient* and *Sacred Hunger*.

10. **Give Me Five** – In Beatrix Potter's original '23 Tales', nine Christian names appear in the titles. Name five (just the Christian names) for 5 points.

**Round 2, Part A) First Lines** – Can you name the book and the author from the first line? I will give you the year of publication as well. A point for the author and a point for the title:

11. 'All happy families are alike; each unhappy family is unhappy in its own way', 1877
12. 'On those cloudy days, Robert Neville was never sure when sunset came, and sometimes they were in the streets before he could get back', 1954
13. 'You better not never tell nobody but God', 1982
14. 'As Gregor Samsa awoke one morning from uneasy dreams he found himself transformed in his bed into a gigantic insect', 1915
15. 'It was the day my grandmother exploded', 1993

**Round 2, Part B) Blankety Books** – Find the missing word: there's always a theme and this quiz the theme is ... the seasons. A point for each one you get:

16. *[Blank] in Madrid* by C.J. Sansom
17. *Things [Blank] Apart* by Chinua Achebe
18. *An Event in [Blank]* by Henning Mankell
19. *[Blank] Snow* by Yukio Mishima
20. *Foxglove [Blank]* by Ben Aaronovitch

**Round 3, Part A) Two of a Kind** – I will describe a character and then an author. They share the same initials so if you know one it will help you get the other. A point for each you can name:

21. Character: J. R. R. Tolkien's brave 'Hobbit' from his 1937 novel of the same name. Author: The American-born author of *Notes from a Small Island, A Short History*

*of Nearly Everything, Mother Tongue* and the memoir *The Life and Times of the Thunderbolt Kid.*

22. Character: the character created by Edgar Rice Burroughs who journeys to Mars; a film was made in 2012 starring Taylor Kitsch. Author: The English author best known for the 'Rutshire Chronicles' including *Riders, Polo, Jump!* and *Mount!.*

23. Character: The main protagonist and narrator from Robert Louis Stevenson's novel *Treasure Island*; alongside his mother, he finds a map showing where the notorious pirate Captain Flint buried his treasure. Author: The author, playwright and screenwriter best known for his 1961 novel *Catch-22*, the classic war satire in which Captain John Yossarian rails against the insanity of war; the sequel *Closing Time* was published in 1994.

24. Character: From Ian Fleming's 1964 book *Chitty-Chitty-Bang-Bang*, this character is the eccentric inventor who creates the titular car; he lives with his wife Mimsy and their twin eight-year-olds Jeremy and Jemima on their hilltop farm. Author: The American author best known for his novel *True Grit* of 1968, which has been filmed twice, with John Wayne (1969) and Jeff Bridges (2010) taking the role of 'Rooster Cogburn'; he also wrote the novel *Norwood* (1966) which was filmed in 1970 starring Glenn Campbell (the singer, who also appeared in *True Grit*).

25. Character: The heroine of Philip Pullman's 'His Dark Materials' series (give the name she was born with, not Silvertongue); she was played in the BBC series by Dafne Keen. Author: The bestselling American author of thrillers such as *No Time for Goodbye, Trust Your Eyes* and *Elevator Pitch*, published in August 2019.

**Round 3, Part B) Partners** – Fill in the missing partner for 1 point and name the author for another point:

26. *The Old Man and the* what?, 1952
27. *The Snail and the* what?, 2003
28. *The Bear and the* what?, 2000
29. *The Naked and the* what?, 1948
30. *The Ask and the* what?, 2009

**Round 4, Part A) New Life for Old Characters** – I will give you the title, the author and the year of a book that uses another (deceased) author's work. Just name the original author for a point!

31. *The Girl in the Spider's Web* by David Lagercrantz, 2015
32. *And Another Thing . . .* by Eoin Colfer, 2009
33. *Solo* by William Boyd, 2013
34. *Closed Casket* by Sophie Hannah, 2016
35. *The Black-Eyed Blonde* by John Banville, 2014

**Round 4, Part B) Literature Links and Lists** – Answer these novel conundrums for a point each:

36. What award links *Stoner* by John Williams, *The Miniaturist* by Jessie Burton, *The Essex Serpent* by Sarah Perry and *Normal People* by Sally Rooney?
37. What do the following literary characters all have in common: Rudy Baylor, Reggie Love, Jake Tyler Brigance and Mitch McDeere?
38. What links Alice Walker, Kingsley Amis and Stephen King?
39. What comes next in this list: *A Stranger at Green Knowe, The River at Green Knowe, The Chimneys of Green Knowe . . .*?

40. What is the link between H. E. Bates's novella of 1958, featuring 'Pop Larkin', Cressida Cowell's character Emily, the character from Catch-22 with the duplicated name and Anne Brontë's debut novel?

Finally, there are six 'SayWhatYouSee' visual representations of novels. Give yourself a point for the author and a point for the title.

Total up your answers and see how many you scored.
   The highest score possible on this quiz is 71.
   Thanks for playing!

# The Answers

1.  A) *Mr Nice*, 1996 (*Mr Loverman*, 2013, *Mr Unbelievable*, 2010)*
2.  Martina Cole
3.  C) *Robinson Crusoe* by Daniel Defoe
4.  Beryl Bainbridge (she appeared briefly in *Coronation Street* in 1961)
5.  B) *Revolver* (this is a book by Marcus Sedgwick)†
6.  'O, what a panic's in thy breastie!'
7.  B) Defoe attempted to profit from civets‡
8.  *Mary Poppins* by P. L. Travers
9.  1992
10. Peter, Benjamin, Jeremy, Tom, Jemima, Samuel, Timmy, Johnny, Cecily
11. *Anna Karenina* by Leo Tolstoy
12. *I Am Legend* by Richard Matheson
13. *The Colour Purple* by Alice Walker
14. *The Metamorphosis* by Franz Kafka
15. *The Crow Road* by Iain Banks
16. *Winter*
17. *Fall*

* In 2019 Chris Kamara continued his onslaught on the arts with his first album, *Here's to Christmas* – 'Unbelievable, Jeff.'
† All these Ian Rankin books share their names with Rolling Stones LPs; *Revolver* is by the Beatles.
‡ Sterne was only eighteen at the time of Defoe's death and did not publish anything until 1743 – twelve years after Defoe had passed away.

18. *Autumn*
19. *Spring*
20. *Summer*
21. Bilbo Baggins and Bill Bryson
22. John Carter and Jilly Cooper
23. Jim Hawkins and Joseph Heller
24. Caractacus Pott and Charles Portis*
25. Lyra Belacqua and Linwood Barclay
26. *The Old Man and the Sea* by Ernest Hemingway
27. *The Snail and the Whale* by Julia Donaldson and Axel Scheffler
28. *The Bear and the Dragon* – Tom Clancy
29. *The Naked and the Dead* by Norman Mailer
30. *The Ask and the Answer* by Patrick Ness
31. Stieg Larsson – this a continuation of the 'Millennium' series featuring Lisbeth Salander
32. Douglas Adams – this is the sixth instalment of *The Hitchhiker's Guide to the Galaxy* 'trilogy'
33. Ian Fleming – this is a James Bond continuation novel
34. Agatha Christie – this is one of four Hercule Poirot novels that Hannah has penned
35. Raymond Chandler – this is a Philip Marlowe mystery
36. Waterstones Book of the Year
37. They are all lawyers in John Grisham novels
38. They all have children who are published authors: Rebecca Walker, Martin Amis and Joe Hill
39. *The Children of Green Knowe*: these are the 'Green Knowe' novels by Lucy M. Boston from the fourth in reverse publication order
40. British Prime Ministers: H. E. Bates's *Darling Buds of **May***, Cressida Cowell's *Emily **Brown***, '**Major** Major' from *Catch-22* and Anne Brontë's *Agnes **Grey***

---

\* Caractacus Potts in the film but Pott in the book.

41. *The Kite Runner* by Khaled Hossieni
42. *Paradise Lost* (Pair of dice lost) by John Milton
43. *Queenie* (Queen E) by Candice Carty-Williams
44. *A Farewell to Arms* by Ernest Hemingway
45. *Normal People* (Normal Pea pal) by Sally Rooney
46. *Housekeeping* by Marilynne Robinson

# Quiz Number 21

**Round 1: This and that . . .** all the questions in this round are worth 1 point except question 10, which is worth 5.

1. **The First Question** – Which one of these time twisters was published first: A) *A Stitch in Time* by Penelope Lively, B) *Frozen in Time* by Ali Sparkes or C) *A Wrinkle in Time* by Madeleine L'Engle?

2. **Anagram** – The anagram is always an author's name: LIVERS WHINE

3. **Book Quote** – Can you name the book from which this quote comes? 'I prefer unlucky things. Luck is vulgar. Who wants what luck would bring? I don't'. Is it from: A) *Women in Love* by D. H. Lawrence, B) *The Catcher in the Rye* by J. D. Salinger, C) *Lucky Jim* by Kingsley Amis or D) *Autobiography* by Morrissey?

4. In *Alice's Adventures in Wonderland* by Lewis Carroll, the Queen of Hearts loves croquet and uses flamingos for mallets, but what does she use as balls?

5. **Odd One Out** – Which of the following is not a real Marian Keyes novel: A) *Watermelon*, B) *The Ice Cream Girls*, C) *Saved by Cake* or D) *Sushi for Beginners*?

6. **Poetry Corner** – What is the next line? This quiz the poem is 'Because I could not stop for Death' by Emily Dickinson: 'Because I could not stop for Death . . .'

7. **Fact or Fiction** – Washington Irving's first major work, 1809's *A History of New-York from the Beginning of the World to the End of the Dutch Dynasty*, was published

under what name: A) Diedrich Syllabub, B) Diedrich Knickerbocker, C) Diedrich Cranachan or D) Diedrich Barlow?

8. What penname did nineteenth-century author Mary Ann Evans use?

9. **What year?** – In which year did these literary events take place? If you're playing in teams give a point to whichever team gets nearest. World Book Day is first celebrated and Helen Fielding's first 'Diary of Bridget Jones' column appears in the *Independent* (the first book follows a year later). Published this year: *High Fidelity* by Nick Hornby, *Sabbath's Theatre* by Philip Roth and *Northern Lights* by Philip Pullman. Pat Barker wins the Booker for *The Ghost Road* and this year we lose Patricia Highsmith, Gerald Durrell and Kingsley Amis.

10. **Give Me Five** – The subject is crime queen Agatha Christie: can you name five novels by Agatha Christie that contain the word 'Murder'? There are nine possible answers. Five correct answers gets you 5 points.

**Round 2, Part A) Last Lines** – Name these books and their authors from their final words. I will also give you the year of publication. A point for each:

11. 'It is a far, far better thing that I do, than I have ever done; it is a far, far better rest that I go to than I have ever known', 1859.

12. 'Or so Bill Denbrough sometimes thinks on those early mornings after dreaming, when he almost remembers his childhood, and the friends with whom he shared it', 1986.

13. 'Then she feels a pressure on her hand and he speaks his first words for a week. "Keep going, El," he says, "Keep going." And so she does', 2009.

14. 'At that, as if it had been the signal he waited for, Newland Archer got up slowly and walked back alone to his hotel', 1920.
15. 'He was soon borne away by the waves and lost in darkness and distance', 1818.

**Round 2, Part B) Blankety Books** – Find the missing word: there's always a theme and this quiz the theme is ... bodies of water. A point for each one you get:

16. *The [Blank] at the End of the Lane* by Neil Gaiman
17. *Once Upon a [Blank]* by Diane Setterfield
18. *[Blank] of Poppies* by Amitav Ghosh
19. *The Office of Gardens and [Blanks]* by Didier Decoin
20. *Frenchman's [Blank]* by Daphne du Maurier

**Round 3, Part A) Two of a Kind** – I will describe a character and then an author. They share the same initials so if you know one it will help you get the other. A point for each you can name:

21. Character: This Victorian character first appeared in *Tom Brown's Schooldays* by Thomas Hughes, but was developed by George MacDonald Fraser in a series of books where, despite his illustrious career as a soldier, he remained a scoundrel, a liar, a cheat, a thief, a coward and, oh yes, a toady! Author: The German author, born in 1893, best known for books such as *Alone in Berlin*, *Little Man, What Now?* and *The Drinker*.
22. Character: John Updike's most famous creation, he appeared in four novels, the first one 1960 and the last one in 1990 (plus one novella in 2001); we first meet this character at age twenty-six; he had been a high-school basketball star, but finds himself now trapped in a boring job and a bad marriage. Author: The English

novelist born in 1920, best known for his books *Watership Down* and *The Plague Dogs*.

23. Character: The character from Charles Dickens's book *Oliver Twist* who works for Fagin as a heavy and is the lover (and then murderer) of Nancy; he is usually accompanied by his bull terrier Bull's-eye. Author: The German author, lawyer and academic best known for his international bestseller from 1995, *The Reader*; the book was filmed in 2008 leading to an Academy Award for Kate Winslet for her portrayal of Hanna Schmitz.

24. Character: A character that first appeared in Robert Louis Stevenson's 1883 book *Treasure island*, his first name is never stated (so I am using his title and surname here); the treasure that this character buries will be later sought by Jim Hawkins, the protagonist of the book; Long John Silver (his quartermaster) named his parrot after this character. Author: The German author best known for her 'Inkheart' trilogy, she also penned the 'MirrorWorld' series; *Inkheart* was filmed in 2008 and starred Brendan Fraser.

25. Character: The protagonist and anti-hero of Irving Welsh's 1993 novel *Trainspotting*, he also appears in its sequel *Porno* and it's prequel *Skagboys*; in the film of *Trainspotting* this character was played by Ewan McGregor. Author: The prolific British children's author and poet who was the Children's Laureate from 2007 to 2009; he wrote the hugely successful children's book *We're Going on a Bear Hunt* (illustrated by Helen Oxenbury), published in 1989.

**Round 3, Part B) It's Looking Bleak** – Questions about dystopian novels, a point for every correct answer.

26. In which 2006 novel by Cormac McCarthy are the two main characters known simply as 'the man' and 'the boy'?

27. In Emily St John Mandel's 2014 book *Station Eleven*, in which a global pandemic has wiped out the majority of the Earth's population, which author's work is still being performed by the 'travelling symphony' amid the devastation?
28. What is the name of the sovereign state in which Suzanne Collins's 'Hunger Games' series is set?
29. *The Children of Men* (from 1992), which is set in 2021, by which time the population has become infertile, is by which author, better known for her crime thrillers?
30. Can you name John Wyndham's 1953 novel set in a post-apocalyptic world populated by (secret) telepaths?

**Round 2, Part A) Lord of the Rings or Kings of the Discs** – Are these J. R. R. Tolkien titles (including posthumous releases) or progressive rock albums? Answer 'Tolkien' or 'NotTolkien'. A point for each correct answer:

31. *A Farewell to Kings*
32. *The Fall of Gondolin*
33. *Tales from the Topographic Oceans*
34. *Leaf by Niggle*
35. *Tales from the Perilous Realm*

**Round 4, Part B) Literature Links and Lists** – Answer these novel conundrums for a point each:

36. Who appears in the title of books by Ian Rankin, Glenn David Gold and Lauren Weisberger?
37. What links *The Wasp Factory* by Ian Banks, *Down and Out in Paris and London* by George Orwell and *If Morning Ever Comes* by Anne Tyler?
38. What is the link between: Ocean Vuong's 2019 debut novel, Carlos Ruiz Zafón's bestselling novel of 2001,

Michael Wolff's 2018 book on President Trump and the first novel in Andrea Camilleri's popular 'Inspector Montalbano' series?

39. What links *Lovely Bones* by Alice Sebold, *My Name is Red* by Orhan Pamuk and *Transparent Things* by Vladimir Nabokov?

40. What links Dan Brown, Michael Morpurgo and Joanne Harris?

Finally, there are six 'SayWhatYouSee' visual representations of novels. Give yourself a point for the author and a point for the title.

Total up your answers and see how many you scored.

The highest score possible on this quiz is 66.

Thanks for playing!

# The Answers

1. A) *A Wrinkle in Time*, 1962 (*A Stitch in Time*, 1976, *Frozen in Time*, 2009)
2. Irvine Welsh
3. A) *Women in Love* by D. H. Lawrence
4. Hedgehogs
5. B) *The Ice Cream Girls* (this is a Dorothy Koomson book)
6. 'He kindly stopped for me'
7. B) Diedrich Knickerbocker*
8. George Eliot
9. 1995
10. *The Murder on the Links, The Murder of Roger Ackroyd, The Murder at the Vicarage, Murder on the Orient Express, The A.B.C. Murders, Murder in Mesopotamia, Murder is Easy, A Murder Is Announced, Sleeping Murder*
11. *A Tale of Two Cities* by Charles Dickens
12. *It* by Stephen King
13. *The Hand that First Held Mine* by Maggie O'Farrell
14. *The Age of Innocence* by Edith Wharton
15. *Frankenstein* by Mary Shelley
16. *Ocean*
17. *River*

* The name was adopted for the New York Basketball team (the Knicks). Also the knee breeches the character wore in the book became known as 'Knickerbockers' – this is where we (in the UK) get the word knickers from.

18. *Sea*
19. *Ponds*
20. *Creek*
21. Harry Flashman and Hans Fallada
22. Rabbit Angstrom and Richard Adams
23. Bill Sikes and Bernhard Schlink
24. Captain Flint and Cornelia Funke
25. Mark Renton and Michael Rosen*
26. *The Road*
27. William Shakespeare
28. Panem
29. P. D. James
30. *The Chrysalids*
31. Not Tolkien: this is a 1977 album by Rush
32. Tolkien: published posthumously in 2018
33. Not Tolkien: this a 1973 album by Yes
34. Tolkien: a children's story first published in 1945
35. Tolkien: an anthology published in 1997
36. The Devil: *Rather Be the Devil* by Ian Rankin, *Carter Beats the Devil* by Glenn David Gold, *The Devil Wears Prada* by Lauren Weisberger
37. They are all debut novels
38. The elements: *On **Earth** We're Briefly Gorgeous* by Ocean Vuong, *The Shadow of the **Wind*** by Carlos Ruiz Zafón, ***Fire** and Fury* by Michael Wolff and *The Shape of **Water*** by Andrea Camilleri
39. They all have dead narrators
40. They are all ex-teachers

* In 2014 *We're Going on a Bear Hunt* was the subject of a successful Guinness World Record attempt for 'Largest Reading Lesson', which saw 1,438 children attend and around a further 30,000 listen online. The record was broken in 2017 by a reading lesson involving 11,137 pupils on the Great Wall of China.

41. *The Remains of the Day* by Kazuo Ishiguro
42. *Cat's Eye* (Cat's aye) by Margaret Atwood
43. *The Piano Teacher* by Elfriede Jelinek
44. *Bird Box* by Josh Malerman
45. *Bad Pharma* (Bad Farmer) by Ben Goldacre
46. *Pet Sematary* by Stephen King

# Quiz Number 22

**Round 1: This and That . . .** all the questions in this round are worth 1 point except question 10, which is worth 5.

1. **The First Question** – Which one of these multiple Booker Prize winners was born first: A) Hilary Mantel, B) Margaret Atwood or C) Peter Carey?

2. **Anagram** – The anagram is always an author's name: ALONE DEFIED

3. **Book Quote** – Can you name the book from which this quote comes? 'Laugh as much as you choose, but you will not laugh me out of my opinion.' Is it from: A) *The Age of Innocence* by Edith Wharton, B) *Pride and Prejudice* by Jane Austen, C) *The Awakening* by Kate Chopin or D) *The Purple Revolution* by Nigel Farage?

4. *Ariel* by André Maurois is what: A) the first book on the Moon, i.e. the book Neil Armstrong took to the Moon, B) the first book Penguin ever published or C) the first book to have an ISBN?

5. **Odd One Out** – Which of the following is not a real Malorie Blackman novel: A) *Double Cross*, B) *Cross Her Heart*, C) *Crossfire* or D) *Noughts and Crosses*?

6. **Poetry Corner** – What is the next line? This quiz the poem is *Kubla Khan* by Samuel Taylor Coleridge: 'In Xanadu did Kubla Khan . . .'

7. **Fact or Fiction** – Which of the following is a fact about Roald Dahl: A) the school that Dahl attended as a child was sent chocolate bars by Cadbury and the children

were asked to rate the new flavours – possibly influencing his books about Willy Wonka, B) Dahl doted on his pet tortoise as a child, so much so that when it passed away his parents replaced it with another similar one (this happened three times until Dahl realised) – this may have influenced his book *Esio Trot*, or C) Dahl loathed PE as a child and he particularly disliked his PE teachers so as revenge he named the mean, cruel and stupid farmers in *Fantastic Mr Fox* after them (Boggis, Bunce and Bean)?

8. This book, first published in 1847, has been adapted many times, including as a 1939 film with Laurence Olivier, a TV series with Tom Hardy and a stage musical conceived by and starring Cliff Richard, and it was the inspiration for a no. 1 single in 1978. Can you name the book?

9. **What Year?** – In which year did these literary events take place? If you're playing in teams give a point to whichever team gets nearest. Carol Ann Duffy is appointed Poet Laureate, *Wolf Hall* wins the Man Booker Prize and Stephen King releases *Under the Dome*. John Updike, Keith Waterhouse and J. G. Ballard all pass away and the no. 2 film of the year is *Harry Potter and the Half-Blood Prince*.

10. **Give Me Five** – Dr Seuss famously only used fifty words to write his classic *Green Eggs and Ham* book (after a bet between Seuss and publisher Bennett Cerf). Can you name five of those words (other than 'green', 'eggs' and 'ham')? Sounds easy right? Well, off you go. A point for each correct word.

**Round 2, Part A) Location Location Location** – I'll tell you a location that features in a novel and the year it was published. You tell me the author and the title – a point for each:

11. Bag End, 1937
12. The Edmont Hotel, New York, 1951
13. Manor Farm, 1945
14. Darlington Hall, 1989
15. No. 4, Privet Drive, 1998

**Round 2, Part B) Blankety Books** – Find the missing word: there's always a theme and this quiz the theme is … insects. A point for each one you get:

16. *The Diving Bell and the [Blank]* by Jean-Dominique Bauby
17. *The Case of the Gilded [Blank]:A Gervase Fen Mystery* by Edmund Crispin
18. *Boxer, [Blank]* by Ned Beauman
19. *The Secret Life of [Blanks]* by Sue Monk Kidd
20. *The Day of the [Blank]* by Nathanael West

**Round 3, Part A) Two of a Kind** – I will describe a character and then an author. They share the same initials so if you know one it will help you get the other. A point for each you can name:

21. Character: The semi-autobiographical character used by Charles Bukowski in many of his books including *Post Office*, *Factotum* and *Ham on Rye*; the character was played on screen in the (Bukowski-scripted) film *Barfly* by Mickey Rourke. Author: The British author and TV scriptwriter, best known for her 'Lizzie Dripping' and 'Bagthorpe Saga' series of books, both of which were turned into TV series.
22. Character: Thomas Harris created this literary monster who first appeared in his 1981 novel *Red Dragon*, and has been portrayed on film by Anthony Hopkins and

Brian Cox. Author: The English author best known for creating Dr Dolittle in 1920.

23. Character: The tiger that shares a boat with Pi in Yann Martel's *Life of Pi*. Author: The international bestselling author born in Cornwall who wrote romance and mainstream novels; her best-known work is possibly *The Shell Seekers*; she sold over 60 million copies of her novels worldwide, and also published under the name Jane Fraser.

24. Character: A Hobbit from J. R. R. Tolkien's fantasy classic *The Lord of the Rings*, he is inseparable from his cousin Merry Brandybuck; together they join Frodo Baggins's quest to destroy the One Ring; he was played in Peter Jackson's film versions by Billy Boyd. Author: The American author and travel writer, possibly best known for his 1975 travelogue *The Great Railway Bazaar* and his 1981 novel *The Mosquito Coast*, which was adapted for the screen in 1986; he is the father of Marcel and Louis.

25. Character: The female protagonist of E. L. James's bestselling 'Shades of Grey' trilogy. Author: The American author born in 1963 whose 2002 novel *The Lovely Bones* was a huge hit and was turned into a 2009 film by Peter Jackson.

**Round 3, Part B) The Name's James . . .** Which James wrote these titles? (James here could be the first name or the surname.) I will give you the title and the year of publication. Name the James for a point:

26. *The Bostonians*, 1886
27. *Notes of a Native Son*, 1955
28. *Dead Simple*, 2005
29. *Along Came a Spider*, 1993
30. *The Maze Runner*, 2009

**Round 4, Part A) Russian Dolls** – The second book's title appears inside the first book's title. Have a point for each book you can name. I will give you the authors and the initials of the first title:

31. Ann Cleeves TGR and Emma Donoghue
32. Pierre Boulle TBOTRK and Iain Banks
33. James Ellroy WJ and Toni Morrison
34. John Irving TCHR and Jodi Picoult
35. H. G. Wells TIODM and Victoria Hislop

**Round 4, Part B) Literature Links and Lists** – Answer these novel conundrums for a point each:

36. What links *The Pale King* by David Foster Wallace, *The Love of the Last Tycoon* by F. Scott Fitzgerald and *The Mystery of Edwin Drood* by Charles Dickens?
37. Fill in the blank in this list of three pairs: 'Obelix and Dogmatix', 'Dorothy and Toto' and 'Tintin and [blank]'.
38. What links *The Pigeon* by Patrick Süskind, *The Hare with Amber Eyes* by Edmund de Waal and *The Elegance of the Hedgehog'* by Muriel Barbery?
39. Name the link between James Henry Trotter, Matilda Wormword and George Kranky?
40. What comes next in this list: *Sense and Sensibility*, *Pride and Prejudice*, *Mansfield Park* . . .?

Finally, there are six 'SayWhatYouSee' visual representations of novels. Give yourself a point for the author and a point for the title.

Total up your answers and see how many you scored.
    The highest score possible on this quiz is 71.
    Thanks for playing!

YOU HAVE A 10.30 MEETING WITH MR. JONES. THEN LUNCH AT 12 WITH YOUR WIFE. THEN...

# The Answers

1. A) Margaret Atwood, 1939 (Peter Carey, 1943, Hilary Mantel, 1952)
2. Daniel Defoe
3. B) *Pride and Prejudice* by Jane Austen
4. B) It was the first Penguin book
5. B) *Cross Her Heart* (this is a Sarah Pinborough novel)
6. 'A stately pleasure-dome decree'
7. A) Dahl's school was sent chocolates by Cadbury for the children to test*
8. *Wuthering Heights* by Emily Brontë†
9. 2009
10. a, am, anywhere, are, be, boat, box, car, could, dark, do, eat, fox, goat, good, here, house, I, if, in, let, like, may, me, mouse, not, on, or, rain, Sam, say, see, so, thank, that, the, them, there, they, train, tree, try, will, with, would, you
11. *The Hobbit* by J. R. R. Tolkien (*The Lord of the Rings: The Fellowship of the Ring* was published in 1954)
12. *The Catcher in the Rye* by J. D. Salinger
13. *Animal Farm* by George Orwell
14. *The Remains of the Day* by Kazuo Ishiguro
15. *Harry Potter and the Philosopher's Stone* by J. K. Rowling
16. *Butterfly*
17. *Fly*
18. *Beetle*

* Around the same time Cadbury and Rowntree would send spies into each other's factories to try and steal recipes – again this may have influenced Dahl's plot.

† Cliff Richard was fifty-six when he played Heathcliff.

19. *Bees*
20. *Locust*
21. Henry Chinaski and Helen Cresswell
22. Hannibal Lecter and Hugh Lofting
23. Richard Parker and Rosamunde Pilcher
24. Peregrin (or Pippin) Took and Paul Theroux
25. Anastasia Steele and Alice Sebold
26. Henry James
27. James Baldwin
28. Peter James
29. James Patterson
30. James Dashner
31. *The Glass Room* and *Room*
32. *The Bridge Over the River Kwai* and *The Bridge**
33. *White Jazz* and *Jazz*
34. *The Cider House Rules* and *House Rules*
35. *The Island of Doctor Moreau* and *The Island*
36. They are all unfinished novels
37. Snowy: these are all famous dogs and their owners
38. They are all set in Paris
39. They are characters created by Roald Dahl
40. *Emma*: the order of Jane Austen novels published in her lifetime; *Northanger Abbey*, *Persuasion* and *Lady Susan* were all published posthumously
41. *The Hobbit* by J.R.R. Tolkien
42. *Shooting an Elephant* by George Orwell
43. *The Riddle of the Sands* by Erksine Childers
44. *Strangers on a Train* by Patricia Highsmith
45. *Murder on the Links* (Murder of Crows on the Lynx) by Agatha Christie
46. *Turtle Diary* by Russell Hoban

* The title of the film was changed to *Bridge on the River Kwai*. Pierre Boulle also wrote *Planet of the Apes*.

# Quiz Number 23

**Round 1: This and That . . .** all the questions in this round are worth 1 point except question 10, which is worth 5.

1. **The First Question** – Which of these graphic novels was published first: A) *Batman: The Dark Knight Returns* by Frank Miller, B) *From Hell* by Alan Moore and Eddie Campbell or C) *The Complete Maus* by Art Spiegelman?
2. **Anagram** – The anagram is always an author's name: THIN MACHO CLERIC
3. **Book Quote** – Can you name the book from which this quote comes? 'Travel far enough, you meet yourself.' Is it from: A) *Oh, the Places You'll Go!* by Dr Seuss, B) *Life of Pi* by Yann Martel, C) *Cloud Atlas* by David Mitchell or D) *Walking to Hollywood* by Will Self?
4. Which Enid Blyton character was described in *Encounter* magazine in 1958 as 'the most egocentric, joyless, snivelling and pious anti-hero in the history of British fiction'?
5. **Odd One Out** – Which of the following is not a real Anne Rice novel from her 'Vampire Chronicles': A) *Interview with the Vampire*, B) *The Vampire Armand*, C) *The Vampire's Assistant* or D) *The Queen of the Damned*?
6. **Poetry Corner** – What is the next line? This quiz the poem is 'Sea Fever' by John Masefield: 'I must go down to the seas again, to the lonely sea and the sky . . .'
7. **Fact or Fiction** – Which of the following is a fact about Douglas Adams: A) Douglas Adams was close friends with Pink Floyd guitarist Dave Gilmour and he even

chose the name for their 1994 album *The Division Bell*, B) Douglas Adams was close friends with John Cleese and even cameoed in the *Fawlty Towers* episode 'The Kipper and the Corpse' as the corpse or C) Douglas Adams was close friends with the artist David Hockney; Adams asked Hockney to provide the voice of Marvin the Paranoid Android for the BBC radio series of *Hitchhiker's*, but Hockney declined?

8. Which snooker player has released thrillers named *Double Kiss* and *Framed*?

9. **What Year?** – In which year did these literary events take place? If you're playing in teams give a point to whichever team gets nearest. Published this year: Sue Townsend's comic masterpiece *The Secret Diary of Adrian Mole, aged 13¾*, Alan Moore and David Lloyd's *V for Vendetta* and Alice Walker's *The Colour Purple*. Philip K. Dick dies in the same year that sees Ridley Scott release his film *Blade Runner* (loosely based on Dick's *Do Androids Dream of Electric Sheep?*). Ayn Rand also passes away and Thomas Keneally wins the Man Booker Prize for *Schindler's Ark*.

10. **Give Me Five** – We'll end as we began with Roger Hargreaves's 'Mr Men and Little Misses' series. There are sixteen beginning with S. Can you name five for 5 points?

**Round 2, Part A) Initially Knowns As . . .** – Authors known by their initials and their surname. I'll tell you what the initials stand for and give you their year of birth. Just tell me the surname for a point:

11. Alan Alexander, 1882
12. Wystan Hugh, 1907
13. James Graham, 1930
14. Vidiadhar Surajprasad, 1932
15. Antonia Susan – 1936

**Round 2, Part B) Blankety Books** – Find the missing word: there's always a theme and this quiz the theme is … American states. A point for each one you get:

16. *[Blank] Black* by Esi Edugyan
17. *Bleeding [Blank]* by Sara Paretsky
18. *Letters from [Blank]* by Mark Twain
19. *[Blank] Ranger* by James Patterson and Andrew Bourelle
20. *Looking for [Blank]* by John Green

**Round 3, Part A) Two of a Kind** – I will describe a character and then an author. They share the same initials so if you know one it will help you get the other. A point for each you can name:

21. Character: This is the name of both the grandfather and the grandson in Charles Dickens's novel of 1844 – the name also appears in the title; raised by his grandfather, at the beginning of the novel this character is then disinherited by him and takes up an apprenticeship with Seth Pecksniff. Author: The bestselling British crime author, best known for her gritty gangland tales such as *Dangerous Lady*, *The Runaway* and *The Take*.
22. Character: The detective chief inspector from Caroline Graham's 'Midsomer Murders' series of novels; the character was played on television by John Nettles until 2011. Author: The actor best known for portraying the fourth incarnation of Doctor Who, who released his autobiography *Who on Earth Is …* in 1997 and a short novel in 1999 entitled *The Boy Who Kicked Pigs*; he returned to writing in 2019, co-authoring *Doctor Who: Scratchman* with James Goss from his own original idea.
23. Character: The titular character from Australian singer Nick Cave's second novel, this character is a middle-aged

travelling salesman, a womaniser and alcoholic who heads out on a road trip around Brighton with his son after the death of his wife. Author: The author, historian and journalist best known for his non-fiction such as *Agent Zigzag: The True Wartime Story of Eddie Chapman: Lover Betrayer, Hero, Spy* and *A Spy Among Friends: Kim Philby and the Great Betrayal.*

24. Character: Created by Ian Rankin, the Edinburgh-based detective who first appeared in the 1987 novel *Knots and Crosses*; he has been played on TV by John Hannah and Ken Stott. Author: The Dominica-born author probably best known for her 1966 work *Wide Sargasso Sea.*

25. Character: And finally, Agatha Christie's Belgian sleuth with the distinctive moustache. Author: The playwright who has a theatre in London named after him, he is perhaps best known for plays such as *The Birthday Party* and *Betrayal* but he also wrote screenplays, including adapting *The French Lieutenant's Woman* for the big screen.

**Round 3, Part B) Table Booked** – Food and chefs in literature. A point for each correct answer:

26. What kind of tomatoes feature in the title of the 1987 book by Fannie Flagg?

27. Name the 2014 debut by Simon Wroe set in the fast-paced and treacherous world of a restaurant kitchen.

28. In which Iris Murdoch novel does the character Charles Arrowby feast on anchovy paste on hot buttered toast, baked beans, kidney beans, celery, tomatoes, lemon juice and olive oil?

29. Which Margaret Atwood novel features the character Marian MacAlpin, who cannot eat once she is engaged to be married?

30. Which novel by Nora Ephron is about the breakup of a cookbook author's marriage?

**Round 4, Part A) Definitive Definition –** One word, three definitions: which is correct? A point for every true definition you spot:

31. And the word is ... 'Parzival', but is it: A) the name of the lion in Rod Campbell's kids classic *Dear Zoo*, B) the name of the planet where Robert Jordan set his epic series of high fantasy novels 'The Wheel of Time' or C) the name Wade Owen Watts chooses in Ernest Cline's *Ready Player One* for his character while logged into the virtual reality world of OASIS?
32. And the word is ... 'HelthWyzer', but is it: A) the first sugar-free sweet ever made, as featured in Roald Dahl's *Charlie and the Great Glass Elevator*, B) a compound that Jimmy (aka 'Snowman') attends in Margaret Atwood's *Oryx and Crake* or C) in *Asterix and the Big Fight*, a rival druid hired by the Romans to aid their attempt to unseat the village chief Vitalstatistix?
33. And the word is ... 'Barometz', but is it: A) the name of the head creature in Maurice Sendak's *Where the Wild Things Are*, B) the name of the escape capsule (never used) on board the *Nautilus*, Captain Nemo's submarine in Jules Verne's *Twenty Thousand Leagues Under the Sea* or C) a plant in the shape of a lamb in Jorge Luis Borges's 1957 work, *The Book of Imaginary Beings*?
34. And the word is ... 'Frithrah', but is it: A) an exclamation made by the rabbits in Richard Adams's *Watership Down*, B) the ancient enemy of Ramses in Anne Rice's *The Mummy, or Ramses the Damned* or C) the name of the protagonist, a vacuum cleaner salesman who

becomes involved with MI6 and is sent to Havana, in Graham Greene's novel *Our Man in Havana*?

35. And the word is ... 'Barsoom', but is it: A) the 'Gentlemen's Club' where Bruce Robertson fritters away his time and money in Irving Welsh's novel *Filth*, B) the name of the fourth planet from the Sun (i.e. Mars) according to its inhabitants in Edgar Rice Burroughs's novels or C) the leader of the 'Ancients' – the original vampires in Guillermo del Toro and Chuck Hogan's 'The Strain' trilogy?

**Round 4, Part B) Literature Links and Lists** – Answer these novel conundrums for a point each:

36. *Ulysses* by James Joyce, *After Dark* by Haruki Murakami and *Saturday* by Ian McEwan all have what in common?
37. What bird appears in the title of books by David Mitchell, Jung Chang and Nassim Nicholas Taleb?
38. What links the following works of literature: *City of Glass* by Paul Auster, *Lanark* by Alasdair Gray, *Money* by Martin Amis and *Summertime* by J. M. Coetzee?
39. What is the link between Colson Whitehead's book from 2019, Sophie Hannah's Poirot novel from 2018 and the autobiography of Hollywood legend Esther Williams?
40. What links all the books Robert Ludlum published under his own name?

Finally, there are six 'SayWhatYouSee' visual representations of novels. Give yourself a point for the author and a point for the title.

Total up your answers and see how many you scored.
   The highest score possible on this quiz is 61
   Thanks for playing!

## 1. WESDAY
## 2. WEDSAY
## 3. WDESAY

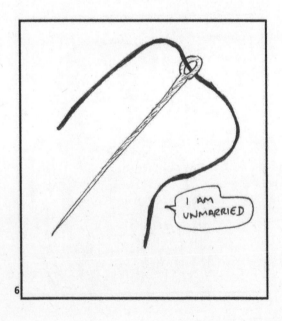

# The Answers

1. C) *The Complete Maus* by Art Spiegelman, 1980 (*The Dark Knight Returns*, 1986, *From Hell*, 1989)
2. Michael Crichton
3. C) *Cloud Atlas* by David Mitchell
4. Noddy
5. C) *The Vampire's Assistant* (that is a novel by Darren Shan)
6. 'And all I ask is a tall ship and a star to steer her by'
7. A) Adams named *The Division Bell*\*
8. Ronnie O'Sullivan
9. 1982
10. Mr Sneeze, Snow, Silly, Slow, Strong, Skinny, Small; Little Miss Sunshine, Shy, Sparkle, Splendid, Star, Stubborn, Scatterbrain, Scary, Somersault
11. A. A. Milne
12. W. H. Auden
13. J. G. Ballard
14. V. S. Naipaul
15. A. S. Byatt (born Antonia Susan Drabble)
16. *Washington*
17. *Kansas*
18. *Hawaii*

\* Adams did provide some words to a book that Hockney illustrated – *Hockney's Alphabet*. Also Douglas Adams (and John Lloyd) wrote episodes of the 1979 TV series *Dr Snuggles* – I didn't feel like I could use this in the quiz but I love this fact!

19. *Texas*
20. *Alaska*
21. Martin Chuzzlewit and Martina Cole
22. Tom Barnaby and Tom Baker
23. Bunny Munro and Ben Macintyre
24. John Rebus and Jean Rhys
25. Hercule Poirot and Harold Pinter
26. Fried green (*Fried Green Tomatoes at the Whistle Stop Café*)
27. *Chop Chop*
28. *The Sea, The Sea*
29. *The Edible Woman*
30. *Heartburn*
31. C) It's the name Wade Owen Watts adopts in *Ready Player One*
32. B) It is Atwood's *Oryx and Crake* compound
33. C) It's a creature/plant from Borges's *Book of Imaginary Beings**
34. A) It is part of the Lapine language invented by Adams for his book and means 'Lord Sun!' (the character in Greene's novel is called James Wormold)
35. B) It is Edgar Rice Burroughs's *Mars*
36. They are all set on a single day
37. Swan: *Black Swan Green* by David Mitchell, *Wild Swans* by Jung Chang and *The Black Swan* by Nassim Nicholas Taleb
38. The author appears as a character
39. American money: *The Nickel Boys*, *The Mystery of Three Quarters* and *The Million Dollar Mermaid*
40. They all have three-word titles
41. *Notes from a Small Island* (Wine tasters 'notes') by Bill Bryson

* Sendak doesn't name the Wild Things in his book.

42. *Night School* (Knight school) by Lee Child (or C.J. Daugherty)
43. *The Plot Against America* by Philip Roth
44. *To Kill a Mockingbird* by Harper Lee
45. *Our Endless Numbered Days* ('END' less, numbered days) by Claire Fuller
46. *A Single Thread* by Tracy Chevalier

# Quiz Number 24: The Christmas Quiz

**Round 1: This and That . . .** all the questions in this round are worth 1 point except question 10, which is worth 5.

1. **The First Question** – Which of these Raymond Briggs books was published first: A) *The Snowman*, B) *Father Christmas* or C) *Father Christmas Goes on Holiday*?
2. **Anagram** – The anagram is always an author's name: AUTOMATICALLY SO
3. **Book Quote** – Can you name the book from which this quote comes? 'Fine old Christmas, with the snowy hair and ruddy face, had done his duty that year in the noblest fashion, and had set off his rich gifts of warmth and colour with all the heightening contrast of frost and snow.' Is it from: A) *A Christmas Memory* by Truman Capote, B) *The Mill on the Floss* by George Eliot, C) *The Gift of the Magi* by O. Henry or D) *A Scottish Lord for Christmas* by Lauren Smith?
4. How many times does Scrooge say 'Humbug' in *A Christmas Carol*: A) two, B) six, C) twelve or D) never?
5. **Odd One Out** – Which of the following is not a real tale of Beatrix Potter: A) *The Tale of Timmy Tiptoes*, B) *The Tale of Tommy Twinkle Nose*, C) *The Tale of Mrs Tittlemouse* or D) *The Tale of Mrs Tiggy-Winkle*?

6.  **Poetry Corner** – What is the next line? This quiz the poem is 'A Visit from St Nicholas' by Clement Clarke Moore: ''Twas the night before Christmas, When all through the house . . .'

7.  **Fact or Fiction** – Which of the following is a fact about Terry Pratchett: A) as a boy Terry Pratchett loved lizards and later as an adult he sponsored the lizard enclosure at London Zoo for five years, B) as a boy Terry Pratchett loved the stars and later as an a adult he had a meteorite named after him by NASA called 127005 Pratchett or C) as a boy Terry Pratchett loved football after seeing England win the World Cup in 1966; his love continued into adulthood and in 2005 he bought a ball from that game for £700,000 pounds at Sotheby's?

8.  Published on Christmas Eve in the *London Evening News*, 1925, 'The Wrong Sort of Bees' was the first story to feature which fictional bear?

9.  **What Year?** – In which year did these literary events take place? If you're playing in teams give a point to whichever team gets nearest. On a train from Manchester to London J. K. Rowling has the idea for a book about a boy wizard. Roald Dahl passes away. Alan Moore and David Lloyd release the graphic novel *V for Vendetta*. Also published this year: Michael Crichton's *Jurassic Park*, Hanif Kureishi's *The Buddha of Suburbia* and *Good Omens* by Neil Gaiman and Terry Pratchett.

10. **Give Me Five** – Name five of Santa's reindeers (as featured in Clement C. Moore's 1823 poem 'A Visit from Father Christmas'). There are eight possible answers; five correct guesses gets you 5 points.

**Round 2, Part A) Christmas Conundrums** – A point for every correct answer:

11. Who wrote the 2003 bestseller in which Henry DeTamble time-travels his way out of a car crash that kills his mother one Christmas Eve?
12. Name the author of *The Naked Civil Servant* who was born Denis Charles Pratt on Christmas Day in 1908.
13. Charles Dickens's *A Christmas Carol* is the ultimate Christmas read for many people. When was it originally published: A) 1843, B) 1849 or C) 1855?
14. In Nicholas Allan's 2009 kids' book what does Father Christmas need?
15. Which single from 1987 took its title from that of a novel by J.P. Donleavy published in 1973? At time of writing it has re-entered the top 20 at Christmas every year since 2005.

**Round 2, Part B) Blankety Books** – Find the missing word: there's always a theme and this quiz the theme is . . . the 'Twelve Days of Christmas' song. A point for each one you get:

16. *The Little [Blank] Girl* by John le Carré
17. *The Beggar [Blank]* by Alice Munro
18. *The Wings of the [Blank]* by Henry James
19. *[Blank] of the Flies* by William Golding
20. *Wild [Blanks]: Three Daughters of China* by Jung Chang

**Round 3, Part A) Two of a Kind** – I will describe a character and then an author. They share the same initials so if you know one it will help you get the other. A point for each you can name:

21. Character: The youngest sister and baby of the family that features in *Little Women*. Author: The Canadian

short-story writer who won the Nobel Prize in Literature in 2013 and the 2009 Man Booker International Prize for her lifetime body of work; her collections include *Dance of the Happy Shades* and *Dear Life*.

22. Character: In C. S. Lewis's 'The Chronicles of Narnia' series, she is the elder sister and the second eldest child of the family; in *The Lion, the Witch and the Wardrobe*, Father Christmas gives her a bow with arrows that never miss their target, and a magical horn that brings aid when blown. Author: American poet, novelist and short-story writer probably best known for *The Bell Jar*; in 1982, she won a posthumous Pulitzer Prize for *The Collected Poems*.

23. Character: The first ghost Scrooge encounters in Dickens's *A Christmas Carol*. Author: The English journalist, novelist and screenwriter best known for her 2012 book *Me Before You*, which was filmed in 2016, starring Emilia Clarke and Sam Claflin.

24. Character: The protagonist from Susan Cooper's children's classic *The Dark Is Rising*, he begins to have strange experiences on his eleventh birthday, just before Christmas; he soon learns he is one of the 'Old Ones', a guardian and warrior for the Light. Author: The author of *Great Apes*, *The Book of Dave* and *Shark*; he released his autobiography in 2019 to mixed reviews; it was described in the *Telegraph* as 'a deliberately repulsive portrait of the author's junkie years'.

25. Character: A *bit* of a cheat – but there is a graphic novel version: so, it's the character from Tim Burton's *The Nightmare Before Christmas* graphic novel; he's the king of 'Halloween Town' who stumbles through a portal to 'Christmas Town' and decides to celebrate the holiday. Author: The Swiss-born nineteenth-century author best known for her book *Heidi* published in 1881; it remains one of the bestselling books ever written; those

of you of a certain age will remember the badly dubbed TV series from your youth.

**Round 3, Part B) It's a Mystery** – Are these Agatha Christie books Poirot or Marple? A fifty–fifty chance and a point if you are correct:

26. *The Body in the Library*
27. *4.50 from Paddington*
28. *The Mystery of the Blue Train*
29. *Evil Under the Sun*
30. *A Pocket Full of Rye*

**Round 4, Part A) Continued Christmas Conundrums** – A point for each one you know:

31. *Twas the Nightshift Before Christmas: Festive Hospital Diaries* was a 2019 bestselling book for which author?
32. Who narrates the 1892 short story that centres on a blue carbuncle being found in the neck of a Christmas goose?
33. Who wrote *A Child's Christmas in Wales*?
34. Which 1935 Christmas classic by John Masefield is a sequel to his 1927 book *The Midnight Folk*?
35. In Allan Plenderleith's jolly little Christmas book of 2009, what titular vegetable is smelly?

**Round 4, Part B) Literature Links and Lists** – Answer these novel Christmas conundrums for a point each:

36. What specifically connects these books: *Skipping Christmas* by John Grisham, *Nothing Lasts Forever* by Roderick Thorp and *The Greatest Gift* by Philip Van Doren Stern?

37. What Christian name is shared by the authors of the 'Geek Girl' series, the author of *Am I Normal Yet?* and the children's author of the 'Animal Magic' and 'Emily Feather' series?

38. What comes next in this list: *Truth Pixie*, 2018, *Father Christmas and Me*, 2017, *The Girl Who Saved Christmas*, 2016 . . .?

39. Name the town that appears in *How the Grinch Stole Christmas* and *Horton Hears a Who* by Dr Seuss.

40. What links a toothpick, a 50-pence piece and a single tissue?

Finally, there are six 'SayWhatYouSee' visual representations of novels. Give yourself a point for the author and a point for the title. The clues are Christmassy but the books are not.

Total up your answers and see how many you scored.

The highest score possible on this quiz is 61.

Thanks for playing!

# The Answers

1. B) *Father Christmas*, 1973 (*Father Christmas Goes on Holiday*, 1975, *The Snowman*, 1978)*
2. Louisa May Alcott
3. B) *The Mill on the Floss* by George Eliot†
4. B) Six
5. B) *The Tale of Tommy Twinkle Nose* (I made that one up)
6. 'Not a creature was stirring, not even a mouse'
7. B) He loved astronomy
8. Winnie the Pooh
9. 1990
10. Dasher, Dancer, Prancer, Vixen, Comet, Cupid, Dunder (also spelled Donder or Donner) and Blixem (also spelled Blitzen or Blixen)‡
11. Audrey Niffenegger: *The Time Traveller's Wife*
12. Quentin Crisp
13. A) 1843
14. A wee! (*Father Christmas Needs a Wee!*)

* Although he allowed permission for the use of his characters, Raymond Briggs did not write *The Snowman* sequel, *The Snowman and the Snowdog*.

† *A Scottish Lord for Christmas*'s main character is called 'Lady Rowena Pepperwirth', which is delightful and almost Dickensian. There are two books before this one in the 'Sins and Scandals' series: *An Earl By Any Other Name* ('An Earl in the streets a rogue in the sheets . . .') and *A Gentlemen Never Surrenders*.

‡ Rudolph doesn't feature in Moore's poem; he didn't appear until 1939.

15. 'Fairytale of New York' by the Pogues and Kirsty MacColl
16. *Drummer*
17. *Maid*
18. *Dove*
19. *Lord*
20. *Swans*
21. Amy March and Alice Munro
22. Susan Pevensie and Sylvia Plath
23. Jacob Marley and Jojo Moyes
24. Will Stanton and Will Self
25. Jack Skellington and Johanna Spyri
26. Marple
27. Marple
28. Poirot
29. Poirot
30. Marple
31. Adam Kay
32. Dr Watson – 'The Adventure of the Blue Carbuncle' in *The Adventures of Sherlock Holmes*
33. Dylan Thomas
34. *The Box of Delights*
35. Sprout: *The Smelly Sprout*
36. Made into famous Christmas films, with a name change: *Skipping Christmas* became *Christmas with the Kranks*, *Nothing Lasts Forever* became *Die Hard* and *The Greatest Gift* became *It's a Wonderful Life*
37. Holly: Holly Smale, Holly Bourne and Holly Webb
38. *A Boy Called Christmas* (2015) by Matt Haig: these are his Christmas books in reverse publication order
39. Whoville
40. These are Christmas gifts from the Dursleys to Harry Potter: a toothpick in *The Chamber of Secrets*, a 50-pence piece in *The Philosopher's Stone* and a single tissue in *The Goblet of Fire*

41. *Nicholas Nickleby* (Saint Nicholas nicks 'LB') by Charles Dickens
42. *The Angels Game* (Game birds) by Carlos Ruiz Zafon
43. *The Return of the King* by J.R.R. Tolkien
44. *Hollywood* by Charles Bukowski
45. *The Song of the Tree* by Coralie Bickford-Smith
46. *For Whom the Bell Tolls* by Ernest Hemingway

# Twenty Tiebreakers for You

Nearest answer wins!

1. How many books (according to lithub.com) were in Thomas Jefferson's collection that he sold to Congress in 1815?
2. The New York Public Library in Manhattan became 125 years old in 2020 so a team of library experts have come up with a list of the Top 10 borrowed titles over that time. *1984* is at no. 3: how many times did they calculate it has been borrowed?
3. According to Marvin Spevack's concordances, Shakespeare's complete works consist of how many words?
4. How much did the world's most expensive book cost (in US dollars)?
5. What is the record number of books toppled in domino fashion (in 2015, according to *Guinness World Records*)?
6. According to Gavin Alexander (a Cambridge lecturer), how many words did John Milton, author of *Paradise Lost*, introduce to the English language?
7. Cormac McCarthy's typewriter (which he used for fifty years) was auctioned for charity in 2009 – how much did it raise (in US dollars)?
8. How many novels/novelettes did Enid Blyton write?
9. What is the record (from 2012) for the most people balancing books on their heads?

10. In 2001 Fay Weldon, author of *The Life and Loves of a She-Devil*, released *The Bulgari Connection*, which was controversial due to the fact that Weldon received a payment from Bulgari (makers of jewellery and luxury accessories) to mention the brand in the novel. How many times (excluding the title) did she mention it?

11. What was the launch date of the first 'Books Are My Bag' campaign (according to its website)?

12. How many pencils did John Steinbeck use to write *East of Eden*?

13. How long was Robinson Crusoe on the island, in years, months and days?

14. This question concerns Winnie the Pooh. Deb Hoffmann in the US holds the record for the largest collection of Pooh memorabilia – how items did she have, as recorded on 8 April 2017?

15. According to an industrious user of Imgur (a US online sharing site) how many miles did Frodo and company walk from Bag End to Mount Doom in *The Lord of the Rings*?

16. When was the first *Guinness World Records* book published (as *The Guinness Book of Records*)?

17. How many copies of *Kiss Me, Deadly* did Mickey Spillane order to be destroyed after seeing that the comma in the title had been left out?

18. Jack Kerouac typed *On the Road* onto one continuous roll of paper – how long (in feet) was it?

19. In 2015 the original key to Oscar Wilde's cell in Reading Gaol sold at a Sotheby's auction in London for how much (in pound sterling)?

20. At 250 words per minute, how long will the average reader spend reading *Frankenstein* by Mary Shelley (according to readinglength.com)?

# The Answers

1. 6,487: Congress bought them to replace the collection destroyed by the British in 1812, but two-thirds of the collection was then destroyed in a fire in 1851
2. 441,770
3. 884,647 words (and 118,406 lines)
4. $30,802,500 (in 1994): it is the Codex Leicester by Leonardo da Vinci, purchased by Bill Gates
5. 5,318: staff from United Biscuits' UK sales team marked their annual sales conference by successfully toppling an arrangement of 5,318 *Guinness World Records 2015* annuals at Old Windsor in Berkshire
6. 630: this makes Milton the country's greatest neologist, ahead of Ben Jonson with 558, John Donne with 342 and Shakespeare with 229; without the great poet there would be no liturgical, debauchery, besottedly, unhealthily, padlock, dismissive, terrific, embellishing, fragrance, didactic or love-lorn, and certainly no complacency
7. $254,500
8. 186 (I've decided not to list them!)
9. 998: set in Sydney, Australia, in November 2012
10. 34 (she was reportedly paid to mention them 'at least twelve times')
11. 14 September 2013
12. 300
13. 28 years, 2 months and 19 days
14. 14,314
15. 1,350 miles

16. 27 August 1955
17. 50,000
18. 120 feet
19. £15,000
20. 6 hours and 3 minutes

# Acknowledgements

Thank you: Duncan Proudfoot at Robinson for asking if I had ever thought of turning my quiz into a book! Also, for all their assistance, Howard Watson and Amanda Keats for shaping and polishing my questions and scribbles, and Emily Courdelle for designing such a lovely cover. And Mark Mason and Peter Hannington for their guidance and encouragement.

I would also like to thank the people who helped me put the quiz on in London over the years: Steve, Tilley and the staff at Blackwell's Holborn; Paul Guided Missile at Wonderbar in Leytonstone; and Richard and Patrick at the Betsey Trotwood pub, Farringdon.

Finally, I would like to thank my wife, Caroline, for her help, her advice and her support over the many hours it took to put this book together.

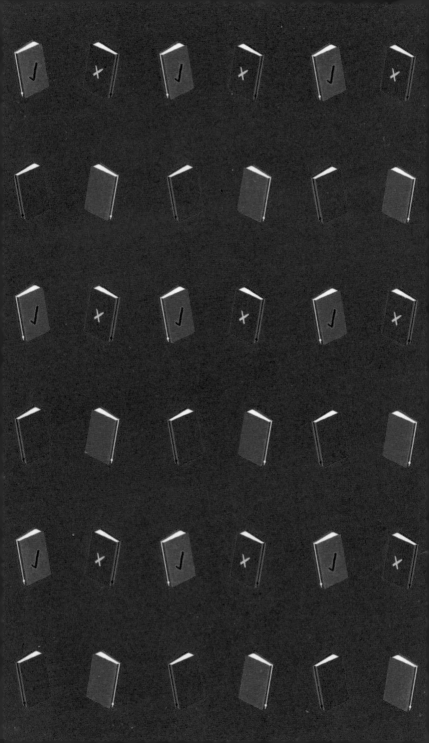